Writing for Others,
Writing for Ourselves

Writing for Others, Writing for Ourselves

Telling Stories in an Age of Blogging

Jerry Lanson

ROWMAN & LITTLEFIELD PUBLISHERS, INC.
Lanham • Boulder • New York • Toronto • Plymouth, UK

Published by Rowman & Littlefield Publishers, Inc.
A wholly owned subsidiary of The Rowman & Littlefield Publishing Group, Inc.
4501 Forbes Boulevard, Suite 200, Lanham, Maryland 20706
http://www.rowmanlittlefield.com

Estover Road, Plymouth PL6 7PY, United Kingdom

British Library Cataloguing in Publication Information Available

Library of Congress Cataloging-in-Publication Data

Lanson, Jerry.
 Writing for others, writing for ourselves : telling stories in an age of blogging / Jerry Lanson.
 p. cm.
 Includes bibliographical references and index.
 ISBN 978-0-7425-5534-1 (cloth : alk. paper) — ISBN 978-1-4422-0869-8 (electronic)
 1. Authorship. 2. Authorship—Vocational guidance. I. Title.
 PN145.L26 2010
 808'.02—dc22   2010028863

Contents

PREFACE

The stories in this book begin in the bucolic French countryside. They wrap up in a crowded, multinational refugee resettlement complex near Atlanta, Georgia. Some are humorous; others, sad. Many fall in between. What connects them is the personal, human ingredient most good storytelling shares.

This is a book for those who hunger to tell true stories—nonfiction stories, their own, and others'. I suspect most people do. Still, many are wary, perhaps overwhelmed, at how to begin. They've been crippled by their eighth-grade English teacher's comments or cowed after reading a cutting Sunday book review. Or their minds have been cluttered by a culture that celebrates the hyperbolic and the frenetic.

Writing ultimately starts with an act of will. It can be a struggle; I know from personal experience. It also can be a joy. I hope the pages of this book convey a bit of both. In them, I'll share a method that, over three decades in classrooms and even longer in the silence of my office, has helped my students and me overcome the misery of that ill-defined nemesis: writer's block.

In the three-plus years it's taken to write these words, a tsunami has transformed the world of nonfiction storytelling. It continues to crash ashore. Traditional outlets of storytelling—book publishers, magazines, and newspapers—have seen their staffs shrink and, in some cases, their doors close. Meanwhile, that amoeba-like monster called the blogosphere has continued to extend its reach.

Estimates of Weblog (blog) use vary widely and are constantly in flux. But as Technorati.com, which issues annual reports on the blogosphere, noted in August 2009, "All studies agree . . . that blogs are a global phenomenon that has hit the mainstream."[1] In that same "State of the Blogosphere" report, Technorati referenced one global survey that estimates 184 million people worldwide had started a blog.

In another report, "Bloggers: A Portrait of the Internet's New Storytellers," released in July 2006, the Pew Internet and American Life Project noted that more than half of those who blog have never published elsewhere.[2]

Some would dismiss this new world of self-publishing with a sniffle or sneer. And no doubt it is filled with its share of mindless ranters and "me-centric" preeners. However, it also offers perhaps the most remarkable practice stage for storytelling ever created.

Starting a blog and sustaining it are two different matters. And countless thousands of teens and young adults who started blogs to communicate with friends have since abandoned them in favor of social media sites such as Facebook.

Yet, in its February 2010 report titled "Social Media and Young Adults," Pew found that the number of American adults *over* thirty who are blogging continues to grow, from 7 percent in 2006 to 11 percent in 2009, closing the gap on teenage (14 percent) and young adult (15 percent) bloggers.[3]

THE PROMISE OF BLOGGING

Numbers aside, the promise of blogs as a storytelling tool remains formidable, as I was reminded again in writing one of the final chapters of this book. That's when I came across a remarkable series conceived and written by Mary Wiltenburg, a talented reporter with whom I worked as a writing coach at the *Christian Science Monitor* nearly a decade ago. Relying in part on a reporting grant from the Pulitzer Center on Crisis Reporting, she set out to tell the story of Little Bill Clinton Hadam, a Tanzanian refugee living in Atlanta and attending an international charter school where he was enrolled in the third grade.

Narrative projects, even those that last a year, are deeply rooted in American traditions of journalism. What made Wiltenburg's different was her commitment to producing it in real time, placing nearly daily blogs at the project's soul. She had never been a blogger or much of a blog reader. "I found them overwritten and self-absorbed," she said. Yet, as a young woman in her early thirties, she knew people who rarely picked up a magazine or newspaper yet spent hours reading blogs and social media posts. "It struck me," she said, "that what worked there was a tiny episodic narrative over time."

And so, even before she had locked in a subject, she conceived a project that would combine monthly longer-form traditional print journalism with real-time blogs, most written, some recorded and videotaped. "My hope was to do something that really followed a story in an intimate, multimedia way that would unfold over time so that readers could participate," she explains on her Web page, http://wiltenburg.wordpress.com.

Titled "Little Bill Clinton, A School Year in the Life of a New American," the project was awarded a 2008 first prize by the National Education Writers Association. It's excerpted in chapter 13 of this book.

Wiltenburg finished the project with a newfound respect for blogging and its role in storytelling. "I loved doing the blog and the stories," she recalls. "There was so much that you couldn't put in the stories. . . . It was wonderful to have [the blog] for all the small moments. It was a place I could cut loose a little bit, but also reflect."

It was also a place she could connect with her readers. Here is one of the series' early blogs, about the day she met Dawami Lenguyanga, Bill's Rwandan-born mother and a central figure in the series.

> I had known Bill's mom for three hours when I asked her if she had friends in Atlanta.
>
> "You," she said.
>
> We'd started the afternoon as strangers, stiff and shy, sitting around with her husband, watching Tanzanian music videos about the coming of the apocalypse. When he left to rest up for his night shift, Dawami got chatty. . . .
>
> In Tanzania she had had friends, she explained, but "Atlanta one-and-half year no friend. Now you friend."
>
> She grinned, and I thanked her, and put my hand over my heart.
>
> And though I've since learned that she does have one or two other women friends here—they're African, so she calls them "sisters"—and though we've since had extensive conversations, with and without a professional interpreter, about journalism and what that means, I worried then, and I still worry, about the scope of her loneliness, the immediacy and completeness of her trust in me, and how to deserve that trust. Starting today, and for the next year, this project is my attempt to be worthy of it.

If, for the professional journalist like Wiltenburg, blogs are a way to cast aside convention, to free voice, to share a sense of humor, and to open a window on the reporter's humanity, for the new writer, of any age and in any profession, blogs offer a chance to experiment, to master the rudiments of story, and to build and share a body of work.

This is not a book about blogging. It is about telling stories, big and small, and the steps writers can take to conceive, research, shape, and craft them. It draws from conventional articles and from essays; my own on those sun-drenched hillsides of Aix-en-Provence and elsewhere; and those of others, from former students to Pulitzer Prize winners.

Nonetheless, the spirit of the blogosphere serves as a significant backdrop as well as subtitle of this book. That spirit removes the sometimes stifling constraints of encrusted journalistic convention. It allows for vignette, the building block of longer story form, that is immediate, vital, and personal. It offers you, me, and anyone else the gift to be an instant publisher, something I've taken advantage of for several years now.

On the pages ahead, you'll find instruction and, I hope, a bit of inspiration, leavened by my own tortuous—or perhaps torturous—personal journey. If the techniques and tips I've gathered over a lifetime as a teacher could help a head case like me as a writer, they might work that much better for you, especially with the blogosphere as your practice field and repository.

OVERCOMING EARLY STRUGGLES

Writing, for me, has never come easily. As a child growing up on Long Island, my brother wrote. I talked.

"You'll make a great lawyer," my mother would tell me.

As I approached my eighteenth birthday in 1967, my father begged me not to register as a conscientious objector to the draft. "What if you want to go into politics?" he asked.

Only I didn't. While my parents dreamed, I had other plans: I wanted to be like my big brother.

Perhaps because of this tenuous start, I assumed for years that most people could write better than I could. Today, I don't much care. Writing is no longer a competition. It is at long last a pleasure, even when accompanied by remnants of pain. It lets me reach out to friends, explore ideas, and learn about myself. It allows me to tell stories and, in the telling, recall others. And it helps me think, to exercise mental muscles. All in all, it beats running in place at the gym.

As is my way, the book has taken longer than I initially anticipated. Today, I know how to battle writer's block, but I've never fully defeated it. Without the patience of my wife, Kathy Lanson, I doubt I'd have gotten this far. And so, I dedicate the book to her and her patience over nearly forty years married to a man who, without a dog to talk to, would likely talk to himself.

Special thanks to these colleagues who shared their work, their insights on writing, and sometimes both: Jacqui Banaszynski, Knight professor at the University of Missouri School of Journalism; Josh Benton, blogger, reporter, and director of the Nieman Journalism Lab at Harvard University; Tracy Breton, investigative reporter at the *Providence Journal*; C. C. Chapman, entrepreneur and founder of Digital Dads; Amy Farnsworth, a former student; Tom Farragher, head of the spotlight team of the *Boston Globe*; Clara Germani, senior editor at the *Christian Science Monitor*; Stephanie Hanes, freelance writer; Caitlin Kelly, freelancer, memoirist, and blogger for *True/Slant*; Mark Leccese of Emerson College's Department of Journalism; Brendan McCarthy, a former student and reporter for the (New Orleans) *Times-Picayune*; Jina Moore, a freelance writer; Jeffrey Seglin of Emerson College's Department of Writing, Literature and Publishing; Tripp Underwood, a former student; David Whitemyer, a freelance writer; John Wilpers, a former editor and current blog broker; and Mary Wiltenburg, a freelance print and multimedia journalist.

Special thanks, too, to Ioannis Papadopoulos and John Forrester, graduate assistants who helped with research for this book; John Guilfoil, a graduate assistant who helped with production issues; and Mitchell Stephens and Heather Satrom, friends who read early drafts and offered suggestions, and in Satrom's case, a blueprint for reflective questions that you'll find at the end of each chapter.

INTRODUCTION

Writing a book can be a messy process for someone burdened by writer's block. I am such a writer, prone to days of procrastination, eager to zigzag away from the project at hand to sketch out an essay or blog or to pen an opinion piece—anything, in short, but what I should be doing.

This book began in the winter of 2007 on a single-lane road that wound through laurel bushes and past tile-roofed houses just northeast of the Provençal city of Aix in the South of France.

Kathy and I readily adapted the cadence of our sabbatical there, walking to the market to buy vegetables and fruit straight from the fields. We tucked long loaves of bread beneath our arms, trudged home, and aired the wash on our patio to dry in the breeze.

It took a bit to settle in, but soon I'd developed a pattern. I read and wrote in the mornings. We'd play in the afternoons. The days took on a gentle pace that provided the mental space and energy to write well. I began to gain momentum.

Then, one April evening, the phone rang. Our younger daughter, Meghan, had news. She was four months pregnant and, though not married, excited about having a baby. I was less excited. By our return to Boston in June, Meghan, alone now, told us she wanted to leave her apartment in the Catskill Mountains and move closer to our home. Life was getting busier, tenser, the rhythms of writing roiled by anxiety.

And my book began gathering dust in a desk drawer as I grumpily begrudged the oxygen Meghan's crisis was consuming and fretted about crossing irrevocably into senior citizenship as a grandfather.

We spent July finding Meg a place to live; moved her belongings from Delhi, New York, in a Budget rental truck; bought a used couch and rocker, a new baby bed, and a car seat; assembled all; and waited.

By the time Devon Alexandria Lanson-Alleyne was born, my laptop hadn't left its case in more than a month. But a few days after her arrival that changed. I dashed off an essay, tucked it in an electronic folder, and left it there—until today. It was short, personal, unpolished, and perhaps unimportant to anyone but me.

But it helped ground me, helped ease that anxiety. And, someday perhaps, it will also record a moment in family history (as the essay in the postscript of this book will record another).

RECORDING A LIFE

Writing is like that. It can give you focus, pleasure, even a certain peace. It can record and order your thoughts, release tension. Or create it. Some days you'll feel miserable or guilty. The words will meander. They won't make sense. Or maybe, on those days, they won't get written at all. But whether you are a would-be professional, a blogger, a journalist or journal keeper, an essayist or memoirist, a poet, or a hunt-and-peck typist, the urge to write isn't easy to ignore. It itches. It's a desire you can't keep from scratching.

For me, writing has never come easily. But today, the essays I write and the stories I tell give me pleasure—on good days anyway. Some days I fail; I never get off the mark. Some days I'll write something I like, revise it, try to sell it—and fail again. Still, I push forward. I blog, I scrawl thoughts and scenes in a notebook tucked in my back pocket, and I scratch. And sometimes a publisher sends me a check or a reader writes a note, engaging me in discussion. It's those notes that I really cherish.

Everyone has an ego. Everyone needs money. But in the end I write for neither. I doubt you will either. I write because it helps me think, observe, see patterns, analyze, and converse. It makes me whole.

That's what happened on the morning of August 22, 2007, when I wrote the essay below. It helped me understand myself and the turmoil of emotion that had thrown me off balance for weeks. I wrote it in a burst. Writing can be like that, too. Downpours follow dry spells. The challenge is to seed the clouds before your landscape turns barren, to avoid the droughts by regularly writing something, even if it is not particularly good. Or, as my father used to say, "Do what I say, not what I do." Here's what I wrote.

The first of our family's next generation arrived with considerable fanfare.

Our daughter Meghan, twenty-two and unmarried, called in April to say she was going to have a baby. In May, she called again to say the dad had moved out. By June, she wanted to move home, or better yet, nearby. She had no savings, no job in reserve, just blind faith and us to bail her out. With each call, I seethed. But inevitability and babies have a way of melting anger.

And so, on Saturday, August 18, 2007, a week after moving Meghan into her new apartment eight miles away, a day after she had assembled the infant car seat and stroller, we gathered with relatives and friends in our backyard for a co-ed shower. We weren't expecting the kind we got.

Minutes after the guests arrived—my brother's and cousins' families, Kathy's sister, two of our oldest family friends, several of Meg's girlfriends—my cousin Maria pulled me aside in midsentence and whispered in my ear.

"Meg's water just broke," she said.

"Her what!" I said. Her due date was September 7.

The obstetrician's office seemed unperturbed. "Finish the shower and call us back," the nurse said.

And so we did. It was a beautiful August day, one with a hint of fall. Some of those gathered hadn't met in thirty-six years, since Kathy and I married on my parent's Vermont hillside. So the day had the warmth of both life long lived and life soon to be.

Bets followed gifts. How long would the labor last? And what would the baby weigh?

The following day, August 19, Devon Alexandria Lanson-Alleyne popped out at 6:03 a.m. She weighed all of five pounds nine ounces. As birthing coach, untrained and unpracticed, Kathy breathed and barked instructions, a new experience entirely since our girls are adopted. I, waiting at home alone, was wakened by the news. As I pulled on shirt and pants and sped toward the hospital, I couldn't keep from considering Meg's—or was it Devon's—perfect timing. For decades, my brother Dennis had shared this same birthday with our father, Gunther. Now a third generation of Lansons would mark it on the calendar.

I don't know what to make of it. I'm not a religious type. But it almost seems that Gunther, who filled more than his share of space in life, has dropped in to make himself heard again.

This morning, Devon is three days old. As strange as it sounds after five romantic and carefree months in Provence, I guess I'm getting used to the word "grandpa." (Can grandpas still sip wine at outdoor cafes?)

"Maybe I'll be called Pops," I had told Meghan just a week or so before Devon's grand entrance. "How about Jerry?"

Now I'm guessing being a grandpa will seem pretty cool after all.

I may yet hang Meghan from her toenails, if she doesn't grow up fast and take charge of her life. But then she just may; I'm ready to be surprised.

And regardless, I know a certain magic is about to return to Kathy's and my life. It'll be special to celebrate Christmas again. I'll have an excuse to play hide-and-go-seek. And sing lullabies. And strum my guitar, long silent. And read children's books. And make noises. And play chuckle belly.

I am ready to gain a new appreciation of everyday life. For that, I'll need Devon's help. You see, I suspect that, through the eyes of children, the world has never stopped being a magical place. Fathers just forget.

Grandpas? Maybe not.

Why start with this story? For one thing, I believe that to tell the stories of others well, it helps to start by reflecting on and sharing our own. For another, if I'm going to ask you to reveal your life, your thoughts, and your memories—and I am—I should let you know something about me.

As I finish this book, Devon is in her thirty-fifth month. She walks, talks, runs, laughs, and gives great hugs. She, too, has helped make me whole. I can't help but write about her with some regularity.

A WRITING METHOD

I hope this book helps you tell stories, too, both your own and those of people whom you meet. It is a book for nonfiction writers of any age, whether you're enrolled in a freshman essay-writing class or an upper-level feature-writing class or engaged in recapturing eight decades of a life well lived. Unlike throwing a baseball or dancing in the ballet, writing has no physical constraints. You can start tomorrow. All it takes is courage and practice.

This book won't try to give you ten easy steps to success. They don't exist. Writing isn't a rote process; you can't just follow the rules. I like to say it's not like changing the oil, though on many days it's equally messy.

I do hope this book will inspire you to write and at times perhaps even make you smile. My goal in writing is modest: to convince you that, if I could overcome my own struggle against self-doubt and procrastination, you can overcome yours, too. Along the way, I'll pass along a few tips that have worked in finding, framing, organizing, and structuring stories.

Good writing starts not with words on a page but with the seed of an idea, fed with facts and details, observed and gathered; nurtured with creativity; cleared of weeds; and pruned to grow straight through disciplined thinking. That lesson has taken me decades to fully understand. Actually, I'm still learning it.

But I am a slow learner. I'm confident you will learn faster.

ONE
FINDING A PLACE—AND SPACE—TO THINK

It was May in Provence. Each day dawned crisp and clear, the sun slowly warming fields alive with wild red poppies. For a few weeks, I'd been wandering the countryside, sitting beneath the plane trees of shaded village squares, watching the old men play *pétanque*, the region's distinctive and often theatrical form of lawn bowling. Participants would toss palm-sized metal balls toward a smaller wooden or plastic one some eight or nine yards away, trying to stick theirs closest. Then they'd gesture and jab a finger, shrug, and measure once again which ball had rolled nearest the target. Debate points seemed at least as important as real ones.

If taking all this in was work, I wanted a permanent posting in France—until, that is, I sat down to write. Then, in front of my laptop in our Aix-en-Provence apartment, my confidence, along with my *joie de vivre*, dissolved. I'd conducted some of my reporting in French, a language in which I am barely passable. Now my notes felt nearly as opaque as the potent, cloudy aperitif, pastis, drunk in abundance after any self-respecting pétanque match. Could I really convey the subtle, but central, place of this game in Provençal culture?

I sketched a rough outline, wrote a few flat first lines, and found myself in a familiar place: stuck.

I had options. I could contemplate my computer keyboard until something struck me (serious writing, any serious writer will tell you, demands the discipline to stick with it). I could panic, an approach I'd perfected early in my reporting career. Or, on this beautiful late spring day, I could head for the beach. I headed for the beach.

Certainly, soaking in the temperate Mediterranean Sea during one of the last days of our sabbatical sounded more comforting than staring or screaming at my computer.

But I drove south with a more high-minded sense of purpose as well. I knew from experience that carving the space to think often eases my writer's block.

1

Sit me in front of a screen and I'm prone to fall into what I call "repetitive stress writing." It is noninsurable illness, triggered when the brain shuts down and fingers type the same sentences over and over. Set me in motion—on foot, on a bike, or in a car—and my thoughts often sort themselves out.

It works something like this: if I can coax my conscious self to close the shades, to place a hand-lettered "out wandering" sign in the window, my subconscious muse stands a much better chance of surfacing to help me solve a story's problems. (A writing coach I know calls this "rehearsal," which sounds so much better than "wasting time.")

GET DOWN AN OUTLINE

And so, I headed to the coastal village of Cassis, parked along the shore, and walked. Twenty minutes later, as I gazed out at the reddish-gray cliffs rising from the sea, the puzzle pieces of my story started shifting into place. I pulled a notebook from my pocket and sketched a new outline. It started like this:

1. Opening scene: the old guys play pétanque in Tholonet.
2. Introduce the cop's son (Alain Gimenez) through his quote on game ("visit any village in the South of France, etc.").
3. Set up game's cultural role.
4. Use Alain's childhood experience to develop point and story . . . and so on.

I didn't jot down much. But the next day, writing made more sense. And though the article changed several times again before it ran in the *Christian Science Monitor*, it didn't stray that far from the outline I'd scribbled during that walk. Here's how the story began:

> **Aix-en-Provence, France**—On a hard, rutted courtyard in the village of Le Tholonet, beside a shaded patio where the Impressionist Paul Cezanne lunched with friends, the Provençals play pétanque.
>
> White-haired men and a smattering of women stand beneath the broad plane trees, tossing silver metal balls toward brightly colored smaller ones yards away. Then they cluster in tight circles to examine their handiwork. They stare awhile. One gestures, another shrugs, a third thrusts a finger forward to make a point. And in the background, someone keeps chattering, a self-appointed color commentator of this game, also called boules.
>
> It's Victory in Europe Day, a holiday commemorating Germany's surrender in 1945. Some of these guys look like they might have fought back then. Two days ago, France elected a new president. But on the hard dirt of Le Tholonet, where nine pétanque games progress simultaneously, no one is

debating history or politics. They're too busy arguing about millimeters—or, more specifically, which player's ball has rolled closest to the target, called the *cochonnet*, or little pig.

It's a scene played out daily across this sun-drenched region: on weekday evenings and Sunday afternoons, on beaches and back roads, and at designated "boulodromes"—from the hillside villages of the Luberon Mountains to Avenue de Pétanque on the Mediterranean's La Ciotat, where the game was invented, some say, one hundred years ago.

"Everywhere you live [in the South of France] you can walk to a pétanque court," Alain Gimenez tells me. He grew up playing near Marseille. "If you stop in any village, you have the town center. You have the church. You have the boulangerie. And you have pétanque."

And where there is a game, there is also the "social theater" that accompanies it. For in the South of France, pétanque is more than a sport. It is more than a social gathering. It's a reaffirmation of the art of argumentation.

"It's all about attitude," says Mr. Gimenez, who is moving back to Provence this summer from San Diego.

The story was a decent read. But it elicited little mail. No radio talk shows called asking for an interview. No one sought to reprint it—nor did I expect them to. To me, what counted was that I had fun reporting *and* writing the piece, something I could rarely say when I started reporting nearly thirty-five years ago.

Author Anne Lamott puts it this way: "The act of writing turns out to be its own reward."[1] Perhaps that is why thousands of people worldwide each day join the ranks of bloggers, in most cases laboring for an audience no larger than themselves, their pet hamster, their mother, and their two best friends.

Words like "fun" and "reward" can't mask that writing—even with a drive to the beach thrown in—*is* awfully hard work. It demands accuracy and precision, self-prodding and patience, constant practice, and the perseverance to revise and improve. It *does* demand the discipline to write regularly, if not every day. But for those of you who, like me, share a certain dread of blank pages, I offer this advice: start not by locking yourself in an office but rather by finding the best mental space in which you can wander. Allow yourself to order your thoughts before simply exercising your fingers.

"All writing is ultimately a question of solving a problem," author William Zinsser notes in his book *On Writing Well*.[2]

GET TO THE ROOT OF THE PROBLEM

You may *think* that the problem is writing a first sentence. It is likely much more basic, such as figuring out what you want to write about, or through whose eyes you can best tell the story, or with what facts, details, scenes, and dialogue.

That problem may arise when you try to conceive of something compelling or unique to cover, or scuffle over settling on an approach that's distinctive and different from the one everyone else is taking. It may come when you try to establish a focus, a single dominant direction for your story or a perspective from which to view it. The problem may trace back to gaps of information needed to give the story substance and style. Or it may have its roots in the jumble of stuff you've collected but failed to categorize and organize.

Rarely will a writing problem begin with the first word. Frequently, it can be traced back to questions about the story's core purpose. Figure out your story's scope and approach (journalists call this angle), sharpen its focus, block its form, and gather the facts and details needed to make your tale vivid, and the words will likely follow without too much pain.

Consider this example. When President John F. Kennedy was assassinated, tens of millions mourned and thousands of journalists chronicled the somber day of his funeral. Just one, Jimmy Breslin, thought to mark it through the eyes of the man who dug JFK's grave. It is that piece more than most that has lived on; it has been posted, among other places, on the website of the Arlington National Cemetery. The story's power was in the simplicity of its words. But more so, it was in the subject, in the human, personal, surprising, and unique story Breslin had set out to tell. Here is an excerpt:

> [Clifton] Pollard is 42. He is a slim man with a mustache who was born in Pittsburgh and served as a private in the 352nd Engineers battalion in Burma in World War II. He is an equipment operator, grade 10, which means he gets $3.01 an hour. One of the last to serve John Fitzgerald Kennedy, who was the thirty-fifth President of this country, was a working man who earns $3.01 an hour and said it was an honor to dig the grave.
> —*New York Herald Tribune*, 1963

Too many writers don't pause long enough to find the Clifton Pollards of the world, the little people who are affected by big issues, or to untangle problems of story approach. Instead, they run straight to the keyboard, convinced perfect prose can paper over the holes in their thinking, the gaps in their information, and the squiggles in their story line. And soon they get stuck.

LEAVE TIME FOR DISCOVERY

One way to avoid getting stuck, I'd suggest, is to cut yourself a little slack. Sure, a good story has a beginning, a middle, and an end. But the process of writing it doesn't always follow a straight line. Indeed, the *discipline* to write a set number of hours each day must sometimes follow the *discovery* of what you, the writer, want to say and how. In a personal essay or on a blog post, that discovery might take place as you first consider the story you want to tell. If you're relying on more than memory, it might emerge as you sketch a road map of whom to talk to and what to look up. Or it might strike you in midinterview, spurred by a poet's stanza, a politician's comment, or a particular detail you observe in your subject's house. (A friend of mine, interviewing the wife of the then governor of Rhode Island at their home, noticed that she served Domino's Pizza for lunch on Limoges China, an odd juxtaposition of detail that said a lot about the first lady's modest upbringing and her more recently acquired expensive tastes.)

Sometimes, though, try as you might to "write as you report," to seize on selective details that encapsulate your story's dominant theme, nothing strikes you at all. As the time to write approaches, your mind remains as blank as the computer screen.

Then it's time, as humorist and author Garrison Keillor suggested in an *International Herald Tribune* essay, to put your work aside for a bit.

> Walk briskly and it will improve your circulation and your brain will remember the basics of good writing. . . . A long walk also brings you into contact with the world, which is basic journalism, which most writing is. It isn't about you and your feelings so much as about what people wear and how they talk.

As much as I share Keillor's pleasure in those brisk walks, you may prefer to doodle or garden, knit, or hit fungos. The secret is to go where you can relax enough to solve writing problems, not merely worry about them. In our overscheduled, overplanned lives, it is advice too few writers heed.

For twenty years, in classrooms and newsrooms, at journalism conferences and workshops, I've made a practice of picking publicly at the scabs of my own writer's block. (I originally proposed a different title for this book: "Tonic for Writer's Block: They Wouldn't Let Me Bring the Gin.")

"I used to write first and think later," I tell my audiences. "That's a bad idea." Writing without forethought, I continue, is like running through brambles. If you ever emerge on the other side, bloody scratches will crisscross your arms and legs.

At these sessions, I share a few of my own scars (unlike President Lyndon Johnson's, none are abdominal). Then, realizing that writers are loath to show vulnerability in a public setting, I take a less direct approach.

"How many of you spend an hour plotting how you'll approach the reporting and writing of your day's assignment before you dive in?" I ask.

No hands go up.

"Thirty minutes?"

One or two hands.

"Ten minutes?"

About half the participants poke a tentative finger or two skyward.

"So you take maybe ten minutes to think through a story you'll need at least the rest of your day to report and write?"

Squirming.

"What's the result at day's end?"

Silence.

"So, when you sit down to write at day's end, how many of you typically know where you're headed before you sit down at the keyboard?"

A few tentative hands reach shoulder height.

"How many of you think best in front of your computers?"

No one.

"So, why do you sit there when you're stuck?"

More silence.

GO WHERE YOU THINK BEST

People talk plenty, though, when asked *where* they think best. Each of us knows the answer. One reporter on a weekly newspaper, a woman I'd guess was in her late forties, told me she loved to dice vegetables when stuck. But the answers shouted back in no particular order are often more familiar. They go like this: "walking my dog . . . jogging . . . biking . . . driving back to the office . . . in the shower . . . listening to music . . . lying in bed just before I go to sleep . . . just before I wake up." They are places, in other words, where people let their brains rest.

My last question is always "Do you spend enough time in these places?"

The answer rarely comes back "Yes."

What does this suggest? If you are ornery—and writers are an ornery bunch—you'll say "nothing."

Still, unscientific as this "research" clearly is, I'd suggest that in a U.S. culture obsessed with checklists, time cards, fast food, and frenzied commutes, we carve too little space to wander—mentally, if not physically—to places where we can tap the power of subconscious thought.

Soon enough, the advice of those stern professionals will come into play. If you want to write something memorable, it *will* take discipline. It *will* take sustained and scheduled writing. It *will* take the kind of care and meticulousness that the experts sometimes refer to as "craft." It *will* take the patience to massage, revise, and revise again. But writing needs inspiration, too. Without it, the other steps in organizing your writing process won't accomplish much.

So, find your best place—and then carve the mental space—to think, to find that inspiration. Set a goal to double the time you spend there. Then ask yourself these questions:

1. What activities help me organize my thoughts?
2. What activities get in the way?
3. What changes should I consider in my prewriting habits?

If it's your thing, the time has come to dice some vegetables. But watch out for your thumb.

Two
A Little Jazz

To me, Provence is old men with drooping mustaches and women decked in colorful costumes, their hair a canvas of reds, blondes, and purples. It is dogs—mops and yellow labs, Jack Russells and cockers, bulldogs and poodles, crammed beneath bar stools, cruising through clothing stores, crapping on the street pretty much wherever they please. It is song birds and flowering fruit trees, fast cars and pursed lips, the singsong of a language spoken with style, the dramatic sigh of a breath inhaled in midsentence, sashaying skirts and boots of fine-tooled leather. It's a frank stare, shoulders that speak, a point punctuated with the jab of a finger. It is the shouts of a market vendor hawking succulent strawberries near closing time; the sharp smell of spice; the tattooed guy, who looks like a bouncer in a topless bar, bringing his love (or mamma) a bouquet of fresh flowers for the midday meal. It's the joyful cry of children playing; a dash of humor; the sound of laughter; the time to dawdle on a corner, five loaves of bread tucked in the crook of an arm, exchanging pleasantries with a neighbor. It is life lived outdoors, succulent, graceful, ageless, and iconoclastic, nurturing, and sexy.

I wrote these words longhand in a pocket-sized notebook, a half-eaten slab of tomme cheese and a mostly drained glass of white wine beside me. This is not a lesson in best professional practices, to be sure. But then, the words weren't meant for anyone but me. We were sunbathing on a Mediterranean beach near the border city of Menton, and I was just playing with words—riffing. It's something I began doing a few decades back out of desperation to burst through all those constipating barriers of self-doubt.

So if you're still feeling stuck, don't panic. If you've already stood for two hours in the shower, walked the dog down every street in town, taken up crochet and croquet, tried chanting, trained in yoga and Tai Chi, and set the alarm to record your dreams—all for naught—rest assured: there are other ways to tap your inner creative self and stretch your writing muscles than finding that perfect place to think.

I used to enjoy writing about as much as I enjoyed my older daughter Betsy's first clarinet recital. Unlike her notes, my words didn't squeak. But as I typed the same ones over and over on the page, they pained me nonetheless. It got so bad that I journeyed to the Poynter Institute for Media Studies in St. Petersburg, Florida, in the early eighties, where I met my first "writing doctor."

"Doctor," I blurted out. "It's about the Ridgewood Village Council Meeting. June 11, 1977. I'm still in search of a first paragraph."

My words exaggerate, but my desperation was real. The "doctor" asked a few questions. He studied my stilted sentences and strained face. And then he offered a diagnosis. "You're not blocked," he said (nothing terminal, I registered). "Forget the word procrastination. You're rehearsing."

GETTING STARTED

I still rehearse today, but usually by design. I do so not only by wandering my neighborhood's dirt roads to free my brain and settle my thoughts but also by scribbling details and descriptions, snatches of dialogue, and fragments of scenes, all designed to anchor my thoughts in concrete images. I rehearse by scrawling short-form outlines, ordering and reordering their themes. I rehearse by drafting and revising and revising again, reading my work aloud to better play with the words, to hear their cadence.

This transition from panicked to purposeful didn't come instantly; no timpani roll followed the writing doctor's pronouncement. His touch of validation, however, allowed me to exhale and try again, this time recognizing that writing takes time and polish, and that first drafts fall short for just about everyone.

In truth, I still get stuck. Writing isn't a seamless process; walks along the shore don't always do the trick. Then I sometimes rely on (or retreat to) the kind of freewriting I was practicing on that beach in Menton. I write fast and reach for rhythm. I like to call it making jazz.

> "Sex drives the imagination, which dulls with age. What does that say about sex?"

I wrote those words on June 13, 1983, five months after returning from my first visit to Poynter. (And no, at age sixty-one, I'm not going to answer the question.)

I wasn't sleeping much back then. I had a two-year-old daughter, a ninety-minute commute to and from my job teaching journalism at New York University (NYU), too little time, and too much white space on the pages of my creative life. My tenure clock was ticking, inexorably, and I knew I'd be perishing pretty soon if I couldn't find a way to publish.

In desperation, I picked up a book my brother recommended, Peter Elbow's *Writing with Power*, and I began practicing what Elbow preached.

"Simply force yourself to write without stopping for ten minutes," he wrote. "Sometimes you will produce good writing, but that's not the goal. Sometimes you will produce garbage, but that's not the goal either. . . . The only point is to keep writing. . . . The goal of free writing is in the process, not the product."[1]

And so, each morning I sat in front of an electric typewriter, tilted slightly downhill atop a table that wobbled on the slanted floor of our sinking colonial starter home, and, for ten or twenty minutes, typed like the wind.

Enlightening, it was not.

June 14
Beat the clock. Fatigue closing in. Air conditioner drones. I'd like to wake up today but can't. Drivel, snivel, Alfred Bivel. Did you know Italian ices contain no spices? Frozen water with artificial coloring can go a long way.

But occasionally, out of the cacophony of my clattering fingers, emerged a thought almost worth recording.

June 16
Rushing headlong without hesitation or procrastination. Others do it; I choke. If I were in the Mets lineup, I'd wear pitchers down with my ritual before taking my place in the batter's box. They might call the game on account of darkness. Gunther [my father] had the same problem. He wrote lists. Busy, busy, busy . . . but the hard tasks got put off until last.

And amid these stream-of-consciousness meanderings, saved in a bright blue, three-ring binder, are snippets of memory that, like home movies pulled from dust-covered basement bins, can still bring a smile.

"The wrinkles around Kathy's eyes make aging an imprint of warmth," began one entry about my wife.

Another, about two-year-old Betsy, read, "Oh but could I wake each day with head as clear as a late spring morning. Little girl does. Always watching. Laughing at us behind big brown eyes. She's got most of the answers already. I hope she remembers them."

None of it got published, of course. I moved on from NYU, and then moved on from college to college three times more before pausing long enough in one place twenty years later to pass that tenure test. But never again did I feel quite as paralyzed by the process of writing. The writing doctor had given me a reason to keep trying. Elbow gave me a means to gain momentum—both by writing free and listening to the cadence and rhythm of the words. Gradually, the pleasure of publishing a modest collection of work—textbooks, magazine articles, travel pieces, blogs, and columns—gave me much needed confidence.

RIFFING TIME

It's time for you to gather momentum, too, to lift those weights off your neck and shoulders and get to work. Pull out a pad or pull up to the keyboard and get ready to riff. Your assignment—today and every day—is to write fast, furiously, and free: words, sounds, or anything that comes to mind. Improvise for fifteen minutes. Hear the sound of language. Make jazz.

And should you produce crap instead of Coltrane? Well, at least you won't feel so constipated anymore. There is nothing subtle about freewriting (pardon me, jazz). It requires only that you set aside a place and a specific amount of time to put something on the page. Let yourself go, uncensored and unencumbered by the demands of clarity, cohesion, or concept. Just write. There can be no excuses, no exceptions, and no days off. Drafting is not allowed. Crafting is not allowed. In making jazz, you're task is to write whatever comes to mind and go wherever that takes you. If it means writing, writing, writing, writing, writing—the same word five times in a row—then do so. That's fine.

If freewriting each day is a modest start, it's an important one, too. At the gym, it takes a steady regimen to develop muscles—stretching, an exercise routine, and the good sense to stop before you get hurt. But the first step, often the toughest, is getting out of bed and getting in the car. It's too dark. It's too cold. There's too much ice caked on the windshield. Why not roll over and hit the snooze button?

For even the skilled writer, sitting down to craft a story can demand a similar act of will. Early in his writing career, author and essayist John McPhee tied himself to his chair to force himself to exercise the discipline to write. Freewriting is a less painful course. To finish the analogy, it gets you to the gym and gets you through the stretching part. It primes you to develop more serious writing muscles.

We had been in France nearly two months, for example, before I published the first of a dozen pieces I sold there. But that doesn't mean I hadn't been writing. Nearly daily, I jotted down musings or observations like the one that follows, which I wrote standing in the street outside the National Picasso Museum in the town of Vallauris.

At the Musée National Picasso, where the master painted *War and Peace* on the ceiling of a snug chapel, photographs are forbidden. Backpacks must be checked. But no one stops a visitor from tucking his toy poodle under his arm as he tours the chapel.

Inside the museum, the exhibits of pottery and painting are well lit and widely spaced. One of the guards has come to work wearing a calf-length leather skirt and leather, high-heeled boots. But in the men's room, the toilet seats have been unscrewed and carted away. The only choice is squat or wait. The Musee National Picasso, you see, is quintessentially French. For this is a country filled with quirky contradictions.

This was hardly the stuff of literary nonfiction. But it recorded a moment, a memory. And, just as importantly, it kept my brain moving.

Ultimately, developing writing muscles requires a more focused routine than freewriting or its natural extension of journaling. It demands that you think and frame, define and focus, shape and sharpen. In writing about others, the disciplined writer also must master the heavy lifting of what journalists call reporting: the reading and researching, asking and listening, and observing and collecting of details, dialogue, surroundings, and subtext that make a good nonfiction story just that. When writer's block brings its own form of rigor mortis to the would-be storyteller's fingers, its root can often be traced to what computer nerds call GIGO, "garbage in, garbage out." Words cannot hide content that's thin, ragged, or unfocused.

On the other hand, developing a daily writing routine, regardless of the content or its quality, eliminates the anxiety of "blank-page syndrome." It'll get you to the gym for that serious writing workout before you've had time to start worrying. And when you open the door, those muscle-bound jocks of serious writing, the ones with the weight of many books behind them, won't seem quite so intimidating.

So get to work:

1. Set aside fifteen minutes every day for at least two weeks to write freely.
2. When you write, keep your pencil or cursor moving. Don't pause to polish or question what words and sounds are landing on the page.
3. Don't look back at what you've written until after those two weeks have ended. Even then, remember that your goal isn't to produce anything worth keeping or building on. This is just one more stretching exercise.

After the two weeks is up, reflect on these questions:

1. When you freewrite, are your words or sentences different in any way? How?
2. How does it make you feel?
3. Did freewriting help you tap subconscious thoughts?
4. Was it hard to do every day? Why or why not?
5. Did it lead you to ideas for stories or essays? How?
6. What does your writing sound like when you read it aloud?
7. Is the cadence similar or different from writing you do at other times? If it's different, why is that?

THREE
CULLING LIFE'S EXPERIENCE

When Kathy and I set off on a trip into the rough-and-tumble castle region west of Provence, I hadn't planned on writing a thing. But our white-knuckle drive on roads blasted through hillsides and tunneled beneath overhanging rock walls seemed a natural way to lead readers into a rugged, historic region where believers in a breakaway religion defied the Catholic Church in the twelfth and thirteenth centuries until the Pope's Crusaders massacred them.

My story began like this:

> **Carcassonne, France**—As we drive southeast of this restored medieval village on the narrow, two-lane D611, triangular signs with images of falling black boulders line the route. I'm never sure how to guard against these rock slides, but the signs lead me to grip the wheel of our gray, puttering Ford Fiesta with both hands.
>
> This is windblown, hardscrabble country with outcroppings of crumbling rock and trickling canyon creeks reminiscent of the dry eastern slope of the Colorado Rockies. Although France has a dozen times more people than Colorado in a land mass less than twice the size, here in the Aude region of Languedoc-Roussillon, one can drive for miles and see little sign of life other than patches of thirsty vineyard and the odd hand-lettered sign admonishing drivers that "Jesus t'aime (Jesus loves you)."
>
> Riding shotgun, my wife, Kathy, pores over the region's road map. "I love these little roads with no center line," she says.
>
> Sure thing.
>
> —*Christian Science Monitor*

Before the meteoric growth of blogging, most traditional journalists felt uncomfortable putting themselves into their stories. Even today, they often confuse their struggle to sustain a sense of fairness with a need to distance themselves from subjects and hide behind the veil of third person anonymity.

But whether or not they choose to write in the first person, those who weave tales, true ones especially, should give readers a glimpse of who they are.

"Ultimately the product that any writer has to sell is not the subject being written about, but who he or she is," William Zinsser writes in *On Writing Well*. "This is the personal transaction that's at the heart of good nonfiction writing."[1]

SOLVING RIDDLES OF STRUCTURE

A writer's humanity can emerge without inserting the word "I," which should be used sparingly. Still, storytellers shouldn't strain to banish the first person from stories, especially those that grow from personal experience. For new writers in particular, the word "I" can help the search for that elusive quality called *voice*. It allows the writer to relax, to strip away the stiff formality of school-taught structure, and to approximate conversation without sacrificing the succinct, self-disciplined clarity of a well-crafted story. Writing from personal experience can also solve riddles of story structure as the writer settles into the comfortable, chronological form of oral tradition. Once the reader is hooked, starting at the beginning and continuing to the end often makes the most organizational sense.

South of Carcassonne, Kathy and I followed the trail taken one thousand years ago by members of the breakaway Cathar religion as they escaped to remote mountain fortresses that still sit as sprawling ruins high above the region's valleys. This route helped shape the story's structure, as we traced the Cathar trail in a single day. The story ended by returning to where I'd started: with my quirky companion and her maps.

> Kathy, I learn, has planned an even scarier route back. As we approach the Gorge de Galamus on D7, she giggles and reads from our guidebook: "an impressive gorge overhanging an abyss."
>
> "I like that," she says.
>
> I grunt and watch the road signs. Red exclamation points punctuate two upside-down triangles. No words. Next comes a sign warning of violent winds and another forbidding trucks and campers.
>
> We pass a gap in the stone retaining wall, where, it seems, someone didn't complete the turn.
>
> And no wonder. The next mile is as much like spelunking as driving. Arches of blasted-out rock form a low crescent over the road's single lane—one with cars moving in both directions. Only periodic pullouts over the narrow gorge with a roaring river way below prevent head-on pileups.
>
> Thankfully, our final stop is the gentler, almost alpinelike ruins of Puilaurens Castle, its path strewn with wildflowers, its surrounding hillsides covered with fir forests. And best of all, the road from there back to our apartment seems practically a superhighway—two lanes with a white line painted down the middle.

I crawl into bed early. Who knows what route my map nut will conjure up tomorrow.

—Christian Science Monitor

Here, a day's drive and a little piece of history served as a vehicle to publish. Writing about personal experiences, however, can be an end in itself.

This is particularly true in the ever-growing world of the blogosphere. My Emerson College colleague Mark Leccese likes to say that bloggers are "linkers and thinkers." This certainly is true in the realm of the political bloggers that he studies. But, according to the Pew Internet and American Life Project, the largest category of bloggers, more than a third, write about their own life and experience.[2]

Many are amateur storytellers, recording a bit of life. Others are professionals, pulled in some cases by the desire to comment on the day's great issues, but in others by the urge to tell small and personal stories.

One of my favorites is Caitlin Kelly, a tireless Canadian-born blogger for *True/Slant*, a hub of blogs, mostly written by journalists, at which I also blogged as well until it was bought by Forbes Media and closed in August 2010. Kelly—who among her journalism credentials has published a book, is finishing a second, has won a National Magazine Award in Canada, and has worked as a reporter and feature writer for the *Toronto Globe and Mail*, the *Montreal Gazette*, and the *New York Daily News*—is an eclectic and prolific blogger.

Among her 325-plus posts in her first six months on *True/Slant* were stories about being a Canadian living in the States; pieces about her sometimes testy relationship with a beloved filmmaker father; one about the lessons of going to camp; and another, written in the aftermath of covering the auction of master conman Bernie Madoff's estate, about her own experience in getting fleeced, and stung, by a handsome con man.

In this excerpt, she shows both her honesty and her skill as an observer. Together, they make for a compelling personal essay:

> We met when I answered his personals ad in a local weekly paper. "Honesty and integrity paramount," his ad said. Indeed. Our four months together became a deeply disorienting, eventually frightening maze of his relentless and complex deceptions and increasingly bizarre behavior.
>
> At first, of course, he was charming, good-looking, funny and fun. He was, in fact, very good company. Until he wasn't.
>
> We met for our first date at "his club" (how he got in remains one of many mysteries), a private Manhattan spot where he sat in a wing chair, his legs stretched out, perfectly at ease. He wore a waxed green Barbour jacket—a classic signifier of old wealth—a crisp white shirt, well-worn but well-cut jeans, highly polished classic black loafers. His short black hair was well cut and styled, his grooming and manner impeccable. We went to a great Italian restaurant nearby and settled in for a long, delicious lunch.

I was at a low point in my life and vulnerable. I was lonely, working on my own, living far away from family and my oldest friends in Canada. Criminals choose their victims. They know what to look for. As someone who's spent her professional life, since college, as a journalist—arguably someone skilled at sizing up character quickly—this would later cut me most deeply. I spend my work life observing others. And how odd, how unsettling, how unlikely that I, now, was the watched one.

—From Caitlin Kelly's blog, Broadside

AN EDITORIAL STAFF OF ONE

Showing such vulnerability in the blogosphere can be especially precarious because it is a world without editors, one in which writer connects directly with readers, without intermediaries to offer advice or polish, without anyone to tell you whether what you are writing makes any sense. Yet, those same qualities are precisely what make the blogosphere real as well as rough. There are no gatekeepers, just writers telling readers what they think or what they've experienced.

"I think people are starved for story," Kelly says. "Not information. Not data. Not gossip. Story." As a reader of stories, she adds, "I'm hungry for authenticity. I want absolutely honest, real emotion. But I do not want a striptease; I want some mystery. I always want to feel there's something more to know about (the writer)."

Whether you wish to blog for its own sake, write essays, build toward a memoir (as Kelly did, using her blog as what she called "batting practice"), or pursue a career in more conventional journalism (whatever that will be in the years ahead), learning to tell stories about your own life will improve your skills as writer. I find it also helps my journalism students gain an understanding of what to ask and look for in writing about others.

Both are reasons why each time I teach feature writing, I start by asking students to pick a place they've treasured, train their lens in tight, and take me there—to reassemble the memory of a single day that has stayed with them."Hear the sounds," I tell them. "Inhale the smells. Share the strongest images. Describe what happened." By doing so, my students practice storytelling skills that they further cultivate later in writing about others, from selecting the telling details that make memory vivid to structuring scenes.

WRITING ABOUT A PLACE

In reading about their favorite places, I inevitably meet the people in them, too. For it is the people with whom we share experience who trigger memory, whether sweet or melancholic.

Amy Farnsworth, who joined the staff of the *Christian Science Monitor* after graduating, was a junior at Emerson College when she wrote about a family reunion in the Ozarks. Here are some of her words:

> We parked the van beside a tall patch of grass sprinkled with wild-flowers, next to the tiny white house where my grandpa Jim lived. There were butterflies everywhere. Black and orange Monarchs drifted like dandelion fluff through the afternoon sky, and I held my hands upward and began to twirl. I remember looking up to see my grandfather's wrinkled smile.
>
> I realized he was growing older, getting a little rusty like the tractor sitting outside his tool shed in the backyard. He didn't talk as much. But he still communicated in other ways. . . .
>
> Wooden picnic tables filled with potato salad, fried chicken and collard greens weren't the center of attention at the Farnsworth Family reunion. It was my Grandpa Jim playing the fiddle, stomping his right foot, kicking up dust.

As often happens with personal reminiscence, this story was ultimately about more than one day's event. What began as a story of family music making ended as one of love and loss.

> [Grandpa] started to play a Johnny Cash tune with the rest of the family. The words escape me, but the melody has stayed with me all these years. . . . That was the last song I ever heard my grandfather play. The last time I ever saw the Ozark Mountains. . . .
>
> A year later he passed away in his little white house on the hill. That night, before I heard the news, I was huddled under my covers, thinking that it would be nice to write him a letter.
>
> I was thinking about him sitting on his front porch, playing the fiddle, watching the world drift on by. I was thinking it would be nice to see the butterflies again.
>
> Today, when I hear country music, I think about my Grandpa Jim, his blue jeans snug over his cowboy boots . . . the way he smiled with his mouth open sideways.
>
> When I remember Arkansas, I see my grandfather's fiddle singing in the orange southern sky, and all I want to do is dance.

Farnsworth gathered from memory details similar to those the feature or magazine writer must draw from observation or interviews: the fit of her grandpa's jeans, the rusting tractor beside his house, and the swirl of Monarch butterflies. These details help transport readers to places they see only in their imagination.

By pulling such images from memory, my students also learn to de-velop character through action, to select details that show, to shape scene.

By teaching them to tune their ear and train their eye inward, I try to instill a sense of what to listen and watch for when they turn their reportorial energies outward (see chapter 9, "Interviewing for Story"). They also learn about themselves.

So will you. Try writing a story that focuses on a single memory of a single day. Tell it like you'd tell a friend. One note of caution, however: don't mistake this or any writing exercise for a license to naval gaze. No one wants to read a treatise on the meaning of your life or a rambling soliloquy about your last year of love. There is a big difference between telling narrowly focused stories *about* one's life and telling the story *of* one's life. The best snapshots in time are spare and succinct. Their vividness comes from plot and detail, not self-indulgence.

BRINGING YOUR LENS IN CLOSE

So, keep your focus tight. Tell about the day you fumbled through your first kiss or found yourself lost in the woods, the time you got fired or faced down a would-be thief, and the tale can resonate with perfect strangers. Describe the day that candy store owner caught you shoplifting, for example, and readers might think about the day they, too, learned that stealing carries consequence.

It is the meshing of craft and self-discovery that makes writing the personal essay a powerful place to start any writer's journey. It forces writers with grandiose goals and ideas to narrow the sweep of their subject. It encourages intimacy, helping writers strip away pretension or a tendency to preach. (What reader wants to spend an afternoon in the company of a windbag?) Ultimately, it bonds writers and readers in the experience that one of them shares and the other imagines.

Perhaps writers shy away from telling simple, personal stories because they, too, had teachers like my journalism school professors. ("Never," they said, "never write in the first person.") Perhaps they consider these stories too unimportant. Or perhaps they fear their lives are too dull—that a compelling personal story must meet standards of drama beyond their reach.

Trust me on this: you don't need to be Indiana Jones to interest others in your life. For three years as a father, professor, and suburbanite living near Syracuse, New York—the most commonplace years of an otherwise extraordinarily ordinary life—I wrote a twice monthly column called "Muddling through Midlife" for the (Syracuse) *Post-Standard*. Soon, readers who enjoyed my stories responded by sharing their own. I'd record bits and pieces of my life; they'd fasten on the subtext and share a connection to their own. Or, to put it another way, stories that worked for me on a personal level sometimes struck a more *universal chord* for readers. Writing can be like that, a conversation with strangers. Here is one of those columns:

Pescadero, Calif.—The fog drifted along the sand cliffs and then slipped back over the sea. I heard the rush of the receding surf and watched as three pelicans flew in formation low over the water, scouting for fish. Today, the empty beach was ours to share with them.

Betsy didn't let my reverie last.

"How long do we have to stay here, Dad?" she asked grumpily. "It's not nice out. It's not warm out."

She had the hood pulled up on her raggedy Glacier National Park sweatshirt, the one my dad bought thirty-eight years ago and later handed on to me. She slouched against a large driftwood log, her arms folded in a sixteen-year-old's funk.

"I miss the ocean," I said simply.

I spared her my other thoughts.

"Curl you toes in the sand," I wanted to say. "Listen to the rumble of the breakers. Smell the salt air."

She already knew I'd been talking about the beach for weeks as we planned our trip back to the Bay Area.

You can probably guess why if you've ever returned to an ocean beach of your past, a place with clean sands, spraying surf, and the sound of children. To me, nothing tugs harder at the strings of nostalgia than to stand by the seaside. The beach was my playground growing up on Long Island and, thirty years later, the playground of our girls on the California coast.

Family lore starts with the story of my older brother's name. He was conceived, according to my parents' best calculations, in an oceanfront cottage in Cape Cod's East Dennis. (At least they had the good sense to take the "east" out of Dennis's first name.)

Although neither of us bears its name, Jones Beach, near our Long Island home, is where we brothers went more often. In fall, spring, and warmer winter days, we wrestled atop the dunes and raced through them with Ranger, our big, black Labrador retriever.

In summer, out at Beach 6, I learned to challenge waves that crested at six and eight feet tall by leaping, arms extended, in front of their crashing curl in an effort to body surf to shore.

More than once a miscalculation left me with a face full of sand or, worse yet, standing in my birthday suit for the world to see as I emerged from the wake.

We challenged the waves in other ways, Dennis, Dad, and I, building elaborate sand castles directly in the path of the rising tide and then scrambling to shore them up against its relentless pounding. The ocean inevitably won; the pleasure came in the frenzy of having fought the good fight.

When we tired of our efforts, we'd stand in the wake, letting the ocean bury our feet in wet sand that slid from behind our heels as each wave went back to sea.

Days seemed long and slow and lazy at Jones Beach. And then, when our kids were young, at Pacific coast beaches named Pescadero, San Gregorio and Half Moon Bay. I tasted those days again, this time from the perspective of a parent marveling at the freedom a sandy expanse gives those in their terrible toddlerhood.

It was these memories that sweetened my walk through the fog and wouldn't allow me to let up on Betsy.

"How about a game of paddleball?" I asked her.

"No!"

"Want to build a sand castle?"

No answer.

"Why are you in such a bad mood?"

"Leave me alone. I'm not saying anything."

Our twelve-year-old, Meghan, and her friend Jessie took off along the dune trail and I followed. Soon it was a game. They ran ahead and hid, and I made believe I didn't see their faces as they plainly peeked above the tall grasses.

"Count to thirty, then follow us," Meghan instructed once when I caught up. With pleasure.

By the time we made it back, there was Betsy playing paddleball with her mom in the mist. Betsy was laughing by now, lunging after balls and having fun in spite of herself. I joined in the lunging and laughter before we packed to leave.

The sun never did burn off the coastline fog our first day back on the Pacific shore. I can't say it bothered me one bit.

"BOOKENDING" A STORY

Looking back, I tried to make this column work on two levels. The piece is *bookended*; it starts and ends around a simple theme: my teen daughter and I circling each other one afternoon at a place we both love. When I return to that opening theme, I more or less resolve it as well: Betsy and I manage to reach a truce if not a permanent peace.

This brief chronology of events frames the column, providing its opening and its natural ending. But the column also is laced with memories, personal yet universal in their appeal to readers who've never visited California and don't care about my family. There's not likely a father around who hasn't fumbled through a similar minuet with a teenage child. And those who've never had children have all *been* children. Most have also had some rite of passage near water—at the ocean, a lake, a river, or a watering hole.

I didn't sort all this out before I wrote, of course. I wrote this because I wanted to, not because a polling company told me to write something that would appeal to water-loving, forty-something parents. No matter what the subject, a writer's stories, well told, trigger readers' imaginations and their memories. The subject matter of a personal essay matters less than the honesty, care, and commitment of the writer. Remember Zinsser's "conversation" between writer and reader. Readers connect first with the storyteller, next with the way the story is told, and last with the story subject itself.

Or, to put it another way, a personal essay is above all personal. It can take on whatever tone and explore whatever topic you'd like. It can be serious or frivolous, revealing, or merely written through the writer's eyes. Just remember that personal essays should be written for story, not ego gratification—that writers can share personal experiences, and themselves, without preening.

Adam Gopnik writes in his book *Paris to the Moon*, "The essayist dreams of being a prism, through which other light passes, and fears ending up merely as a mirror, showing the same old face. He has only his Self to show and only himself to blame if he doesn't show up well."[3]

Writing always entails some risk, but taking little steps helps. Whatever topic you choose, start with something considerably smaller than your life itself. Take on a single memory, and explore why it's stayed with you so long. Think about what image from that memory remains most vivid and why. Then let your story unfold.

1. Try to recall specific details; do not write in generality. Tap your senses. Are there smells you remember? Things you touched? Snatches of dialogue? Details that stick in your mind's eye?
2. Write in small scenes. Think about what you remember. Then write about the memory as it unfolded before you.
3. Write sparely. Verbosity smothers story. Action, driven by verbs, carries it.
4. Like the successful photographer, bring your lens in tight. Start, for example, perched in the tree, the moment before the branch snaps and you tumble to the ground.
5. Once you've grabbed your readers' attention, consider starting at the beginning and going to the end.
6. Save something special for the reader until the end, sometimes called a story's *kicker*. Storytelling, unlike news, doesn't front-load all the key information. It invites the reader to read until the story's central tension resolves, not to get bored after reading the first few paragraphs. It has a beginning, a middle, and an end.
7. When you've finished your story, put it aside for a day. Then come back, read it aloud, and revise it.

Done? Reflect on these questions:

1. What drew you to write this story?
2. Did you start your story with your strongest visual memory?
3. Would you tell this story as you wrote it? Why or why not?
4. Does the story have a central character or characters?
5. Did something happen to the characters that changed them?
6. Do you think the story holds a reader's interest to the end? Why or why not?

FOUR
GATHERING STRING

The best ideas rarely burst to the surface like a genie from a bottle rubbed in the right spot. Instead, most bubble up gradually. They are pieced together by the writer much like the builder of sand castles assembles bits of material washed from the sea.

To see the whole idea, writer and sand castle creator must first collect parts and draw connections between them. That takes curiosity—and a keen eye to make sure nothing of value floats past unnoticed.

Another analogy of how writers shape their ideas can be found in the centuries-old art of knotting string, known as macramé. The macramé master creates striking designs by tying together a variety of seemingly disparate threads into one coherent whole. Writers are also craftsmen; the central thread, or story line, of their creations are often pulled from discreet details gathered and stored in dog-eared notebooks until the relationship among them becomes clearer. Some writing coaches call this process *gathering string*.

A nonfiction writer's string can come from just about anywhere—an unusual sign, a snippet of dialogue overheard in a coffee shop, a line in a speech that seems worth recording. String doesn't wear a name tag. It doesn't announce itself. That is why the best writers take note of what's around them with the heightened sensibility of a foreign traveler who has just landed in an alluring place. They see their surroundings through ever-fresh eyes, struck not merely by the exceptional but also by the unexpected and unusual. Closer to home that might be nothing more exotic than a fresh coat of paint on a tired business or the gradual decay of the No. 9 bus line, a quiet city park suddenly ringing with the cry of newborns or a once-bustling gathering place now abandoned but for piles of beer cans and spent needles. Storytellers are aware the extraordinary can lie just beneath the surface of the seemingly mundane. They wait, they watch, and they record.

Perhaps no one taught me this better than my mother. As a writer, she was strictly an amateur. But the last eighteen months of her life taught me much about my craft. In April 1998, doctors had told her to go home and prepare to die. She had a brain tumor, and they believed she'd live a few weeks. But the tumor, a form of lymphoma, responded to radiation, and soon Mom had regained the strength to go outside for slow, short walks. She began to consume everything around her. She'd walk onto her Vermont hillside each morning and smell the fragrant blossoms of lilac. She marveled as the hummingbirds, their flapping wings a blur, sipped nectar from her sun deck feeder. By summer, she'd regained the strength to walk another hundred yards or so to a brook that crossed beneath her road, leaning on her cane and listening to the water lap over smooth stones. In the fall, she gloried at golden-orange leaves of the maple that towered over the end of her drive. After nearly twenty years of living as a widow who saw the glass half-empty, she inhaled life. Suddenly, everything around her was a moment worth living, a story in miniature worth embracing, a glass half-full.

NOTICING SMALL THINGS

Writers also need to notice all that's around them, to see furniture piled outside a house and ask what happened to those who lived inside, to hear the sound of bulldozers and wonder what will be built in the hole they've just dug. Writers venture forth each day with their senses on high alert—to notice the new billboard at the corner church that reads "gay marriages celebrated here," to hear the high school student who says she's late to school because she is raising younger siblings, to seek out the individual, highly personal stories behind the public service announcement of yet another bike-a-thon to fight cancer.

"Get off Google, get off of Twitter, get out of your vehicle," says Caitlin Kelly, the veteran Canadian reporter who now lives in New York City, where she freelances, blogs, and is working on her memoir. "Watch what people are doing, listen to what they are saying. . . . If you are not aware of what people are doing physically, you can't be a writer."

At first attempt, it may not come naturally, this engagement with all around us. It takes practice to notice what's changed, what's different, and what's new. It takes curiosity to notice the man who stands each Sunday morning on a Main Street corner, with a sign decrying starvation in the Sudan. It takes time to observe him and a bit of courage to ask the question, "Why are you here?"

Practice is a big part of the craft of observing, research, and writing. The Boston Celtics' Ray Allen didn't become one of the NBA's best foul shooters by chance. Every day, he shoots foul shot after foul shot after foul shot. Consider the best athletes, the best dancers, the best musicians, and the best artists you know. I'll bet they practice plenty.

Keep this in mind as well: Most of us are born with five senses intact. Yet, it is the blind girl who hears more keenly and the deaf boy who misses nothing in the bustling room. They have learned to rely on the senses that remain. Those of us lucky enough to have all can learn to develop them equally well—because the seeds of good stories are everywhere.

In the introduction of his compendium of stories, *Intimate Journalism*, Walt Harrington writes, "The stories of everyday life—about the behavior, motives, feelings, faiths, attitudes, grievances, hopes, fears and accomplishments of people as they seek meaning and purpose in their lives, stories that are windows on our universal struggle—should be at the soul of every good newspaper."[1]

Newspapers, of course, are in decline. But whether they're replaced by narrative websites, storytelling blogs, webzines, or new forms of narrative communication not yet invented, Harrington's premise will hold true. It is human nature to relate to and read stories that shed light on the seemingly commonplace struggles—and triumphs—of daily life. But first we must find them. Gathering string helps.

CARRY A POCKET-SIZED NOTEBOOK

Perhaps you are young and have a photographic memory. It won't last forever. I am old, or at least getting older, and words, images, and thoughts flash in and out of my consciousness like a meteor streaking across the sky. I look again and they've vanished.

So, just as I don't go out for a stroll on a frigid January night without a coat, I don't set off on a walk, a drive, or a journey without a pen and a small notebook. Something might catch my attention. Or something might make sense that for the longest time has baffled me. Then I stop what I'm doing and write furiously—before I forget.

As an American living in a foreign country for the first time, my notebooks served a second purpose. They helped ground me. By scribbling down what I noticed in Provence, I started to make better sense of a new language, new customs, and an unaccustomed culture. I filled seven notebooks in all, mostly with material that never resurfaced. But sometimes observations and musings reemerged as details in stories I wrote weeks and months later. Some provided the stories' central point.

On the last day of my French immersion class, for example, our elegant and wise teacher, Marie-France, said, "To learn another language is to gain another soul." Her words tantalized. So I tucked them in my notebook, a bit of wisdom I hoped might come in handy in some future essay. Months passed. The words marinated. Then, my twenty-something cousins visited. Soon they were struggling with both French language and soul as they sought to recover lost luggage. And Marie-France's words provided my punch line, my close or *kicker*, to a whimsical "Letter from Provence" on cultural misunderstanding.

Aix-en-Provence, France—The challenges of communicating across language and culture can be formidable.

My wife, Kathy, and I were reminded of this when my cousins arrived in Marseille from Norfolk, Va., for a week's visit. Their plane was three hours late, their bags nowhere to be found. After nearly 20 hours en route and an all-night flight, they handled their predicament with grace—but perhaps a bit too much speed of tongue for Air France's baggage managers.

In English, they described their lost luggage and called twice the next day, trying politely to encourage the airlines to expand the cryptic message— "tracing continues"—on its lost luggage website. No success.

Finally, 40 hours later, my cousin Steve asked for an Air France supervisor. Could the airlines possibly list the contents of their bags on its lost-luggage website, he asked, repeating a request he had made three times previously in conversations with the airline's baggage department. Then, once again he patiently described the bags down to the frayed ribbon tied on one.

This time, within minutes, the website was alerting baggage handlers worldwide to look for Steve's "knickers" and Hazel's "music stamp."

Progress, *certainement*. But then, we weren't sure the note would help someone who stumbled across either Steve's two pairs of sneakers or his wife's music stand. The lost luggage handlers appeared to be just that.

After three months' immersion in French culture, I stifled a smile. My cousins seemed trapped in the strange dance of pride and language that on occasion can botch the most basic exchanges between French and Americans. I even felt a certain sympathy for the Air France agent's logic: "Is it not better to write 'music stamp' than to confess that I don't know this thing he talks about? And why can't these Americans learn to speak French, anyway?"

So when Steve allowed me to call Air France corporate headquarters, I tried a bit of bumbling charm.

"Je suis désolé à vous déranger," I began, apologizing for disturbing the airline's corporate communications office and—I hoped—demonstrating enough bad French to gain sympathy points.

Marie in corporate called back to assure me that Air France's tracking system was quite *faible*—or so I thought.

"It's weak?" I asked, flipping through the few pages in my mind's highly abridged French dictionary.

As I began to agree, she saved me considerable embarrassment. "Mais non, not *faible, fia-ble*, reli, relia . . ."

"Reliable?" I asked.

"Yes, very reliable."

Marie stumbled again as I slowly read the luggage tracking number in English. Her English, it seemed, rivaled my French.

Nonetheless, she assured me that Air France would scour Washington Dulles Airport, where Steve and Hazel had caught a connecting flight. It was progress.

"The French are awfully proud of their language and can't quite fathom why the rest of the world isn't, too," I explained after hanging up. But Steve and Hazel needed no explanation. They aren't the types to huff and puff about why an international airline such as Air France wouldn't demand that its corporate employees speak English.

I was relieved. Try to use their language, we had found, and the French nearly always show patience and grace. Speak only English and the curtain drops—even though it's tough to master a tongue in which the single verb *faire*, "to do or make," is used in 27,116 different constructions (give or take a few).

On Day 4 of my cousins' wait, we headed to the Lubéron Mountains and, after a two-hour lunch, had all but forgotten about the luggage by the time we returned.

No phone messages. But Hazel checked the website once more to be sure. "Bags at airport" had replaced "tracing continues."

Steve called.

"The bags will be delivered to your apartment," the agent assured him. "They will call in advance."

But what about the four times we had asked that the bags be kept at the airport when they arrived? Steve was too polite to inquire.

By 8:30 p.m. it was getting dark on our narrow one-lane road, and the phone hadn't rung. "They'll never find this place at night," I told Hazel.

She called, then handed me the phone. "Are the bags actually on the van?" I asked agent Anna.

It appeared not. Then Anna offered a piece of unsolicited advice: "We have 200 lost bags in Marseille," she said, "and the delivery service has 24 hours to get them to you. If I were you, I would come to the airport."

I thought of ordering Anna a Croix de Guerre medal for bravery and honesty in the face of confusion. Instead, we picked up the bags.

"To learn another language is to gain another soul," our French teacher here had told me on the last day of class.

I'm afraid my language skills still leave me wanting in the soul-acquisition department. French, as a language, can be quite complicated to sort out.

I wonder: Can the same be said of the French soul?

—*Christian Science Monitor*

DETAILS THAT SHOW

At times, writers gather string with purpose. On the campaign trail, *New York Times* reporter Mark Leibovich watched in May 2008 as the three remaining candidates in the presidential race—Barack Obama, Hillary Clinton, and John McCain—walked the gauntlet known as the rope line to greet supporters after carefully scripted speaking engagements. It was the details—the string—Leibovich had gathered at these events that made the story, titled "Where to Catch the Sights, Sound and Smell of a Campaign," worth reading.

On Obama: He is less of a hugger or a hand-shaker than he is a finger-pincher, spreading memories in half-second increments—about 20 voter touches per 30 seconds on average. He rarely stops for autographs.

On McCain: Mr. McCain invites respectful distance. It is rare to see people lunging over barriers for him, nor will he reach back: his war injuries make it difficult for him to extend his arms. He moves in close, making earnest eye contact while shaking hands. His approach is dutiful, like a Boy Scout mowing a lawn.

On Clinton: Mrs. Clinton lingers, chats and signs her first name—on a Krispy Kreme box, construction gloves and a "Mrs. President" Girl Scout patch (one night alone in Kentucky last week). Her supporters cling to her and urge her not to quit.

Notice that the author writes not of a "donut box" but of a "Krispy Kreme box." Such specificity anchors writing. It helps readers visualize the exchange, as does this paragraph, built from string, later in the piece.

One of the more curious parts of rope-line culture are the various things people give to the candidates: letters, articles, photographs of children, rabbits feet, coins, a Barack Obama action figure (to Mr. Obama in Grand Rapids), a cigar (to Mr. McCain in Miami) and a box of Girl Scout cookies (to Mrs. Clinton in Louisville).

Books are also presented with the utter self-assurance that the candidate will read every word and be influenced profoundly.

Even when string is gathered with purpose, however, that purpose can change. Each day in France, for example, Kathy and I walked down the narrow, shaded lane on which we lived into the center of the Aix, a university town of about 140,000 residents, nearly a third of them students. Our route took us past an elementary school, a *pétanque* court (naturally), a pharmacy, a high school, a bakery, a supermarket, yet another school, and a park before we crossed the circular route around the city's core. Each day I'd pause to look at the bulletin boards and billboards along the way. My favorite flashed the latest in French fashions. February is a cool month, even in the sunny South of France. The billboard, however, was at its steamiest, featuring a model in lingerie, leaning back invitingly, lips pursed. The message below was no more subtle: "Avec moi, pas d'absention," it read. "With me, there's no abstention."

CHANGING DIRECTION

The billboard's message seemed, well, so French—tongue in cheek, sensual, and a bit brazen. I scribbled it in my notebook and decided to keep an eye out for signs that spoke to what makes France distinctive. We stopped at the storefront of Chriss, the poet of Cassis, whose sign offered prospective customers any of 2,800 poems ("a little tenderness in an aggressive world"). We passed a gated home in Gigondas that cautioned "no trespassing" in bold letters and warned of a *chat lunatique* (crazy cat) within. We noticed a Renault in the town of Lourmarin with a triangular warning sign around a red high-heeled shoe, suggesting the driver either loved shoes or stopped for women with nice legs. (Women's liberation has never quite caught on in France.)

Still, I didn't have much. Poorly focused, the piece flopped. I moved on.

Then, in late April, another of our visitors pointed out a small sign on the circular route around Aix that I'd never noticed. "Livraisons tolérées," it read: "Deliveries tolerated."

The whimsy of these words struck me as a perfect reflection of French culture. This time, supported with string to draw from in my notebooks, the threads of a story began to come together. I had been following the French presidential race. The French loved neither of the leading candidates, Nicolas Sarkozy on the right, and Ségolène Royal on the left; these candidates, a French acquaintance had told us, could be tolerated, but not revered. An idea for the *Christian Science Monitor* began to take shape.

> **Aix-en-Provence, France**—The signs and billboards of this gracious city give an interesting glimpse into its live-and-let-live culture.
>
> Each morning, on our daily walk to town, we are greeted on Cours Saint Louis by a black-and-white sign that announces *"livraisons tolérées,"* "deliveries tolerated." The choice of verb intrigues. Deliveries on this busy street, part of the circular route that carries traffic around the city, are not allowed. They are not accepted or encouraged. They are tolerated.
>
> It's a sensibility, it seems, that applies to the country's presidential election, too. Tolerance, at least of personal style and eccentricity, remains eminently French, even as the country struggles in choosing its next president amid issues of economic uncertainty, dwindling influence, and growing immigration. One of the two remaining candidates in the presidential runoff, Socialist Ségolène Royal, had four children out of wedlock and has never married her partner. The wife of the other leading candidate, Nicolas Sarkozy, recently left him for awhile, but returned. Such facts might cause ripples in an American political race. In France, no problem.

The piece ended by returning to where it started, giving me a chance to pull from my notebook other threads scribbled down during weeks of daily walks.

> The candidates' blemishes didn't stop an astounding 84 percent of eligible voters from casting ballots in Saturday's first round, which winnowed the field from 12 to two. By contrast, 64 percent of Americans voted in the 2004 presidential election.

In this country, where dogs are allowed off leash and beneath the legs of owners in sidewalk cafes; where passengers punch bus tickets, if they wish, on something akin to an honor system; and where a scantily clad model on a billboard ad proclaims, *"avec moi, pas d'abstention"* (with me, no abstention), issues of tolerance . . . are sure to influence the election outcome.

Few believe France is ready to abandon its traditions, its gracious sense of time used well but without haste, its sometimes stubborn independence from the United States and its European partners. But the degree to which it is willing to tolerate change and modernize its economic climate, and the degree to which it is willing to tolerate and embrace growing numbers of underemployed North African and Middle Eastern immigrants, could help decide who wins May 6.

Whichever candidate comes out ahead, the new president will face considerable skepticism from an electorate with reservations about both. No matter. If deliveries can be tolerated, presumably presidents can be, too.

—*Christian Science Monitor*

If string is easier to spot in unfamiliar places, it can be pulled in anywhere on any day. Here's an excerpt from a *True/Slant* blog I wrote about my granddaughter, Devon, who in the end bequeathed me with the name "Ada" rather than grandpa. It begins with a short exchange—dialogue—which can be an effective means of drawing readers to a scene and place.

The voice comes from the back seat.
"Do you have a nose, Ada?"
"Yes, I do, right here," I reply, pointing.
"Would you like some pucker paint?"
"No, I don't wear pucker paint."
Does mommy wear pucker paint?"
"Yes, she does."
"OK."

It's Veterans Day, a holiday, and mommy is working. So my best friend (and granddaughter) has dropped by for a visit. Her name is Devon. Though she was a bit of a surprise when she showed up a little more than two years ago, she's as much a part of the rhythm of our lives these days as my morning cup of coffee. And she's a lot more meaningful.

Life often sorts into little routines, patterns that make us comfortable. When our two daughters were about Devon's age, we lived in Needham, Mass., on a street called Bird's Hill. Each weekend day, I'd walk the girls down the hill, turning three times around the telephone pole midway down the block. At the bottom, we'd visit the corner store. Each girl picked out a piece of candy, and we'd walk back up, turning three times around the telephone pole before continuing up to our red front door.

When Devon stops by for the day, Kathy and I have settled into a routine with her, too.

—*True/Slant*

BRINGING BACK YOUR OWN STRING

Now it's your turn. Pick up a pocket-sized notebook, and carry it wherever you go. Or pull out your iPhone, Tweet bursts of observation, or post snippets to your blog. Record whatever strikes your fancy. At first, it might help to seek out unfamiliar places, physically and mentally. Take a different route to work. Take public transportation if you drive, or ride a bike if you take the bus. Read billboards and bulletin boards. Wander at lunch down a street, into a store, through a magazine, or onto a website you've never visited before. Practice being a voyeur and listen intently to the conversations around you. Outside, follow your nose to smells and scenes that perhaps eluded you or passed unnoticed.

Soon you'll have filled that notebook or blog with images and details that spur ideas and make writing vivid. At first, simply record these ideas and images. Don't worry about their significance. Consider this sketching a form of real-time storytelling, cobbled together in disparate bursts. In time, I'll bet, one observation will lead you toward a story worth investigating in greater detail. Another might serve as a metaphor in an essay you've wanted to tackle for a long time. A third might simply make your day more enjoyable.

A few days after returning to the States in June 2007, we joined the French teacher at Kathy's school and his wife for dinner. He had just returned from his first Boston Red Sox game and his first visit to Fenway Park. The game, he said, was confusing. But what had really struck him as remarkable was the ballpark custom of handing money to absolute strangers who then passed it down the row to a vendor who passed back food. I've been going to ballparks with my dad since I was four, and I'd always taken this act of trust for granted. What was commonplace to me was remarkable to our French friend. He might have been on to something, a symbol of the amiable goodwill of most Americans.

Sometimes, details that seem trivial or obscure suddenly strike a nerve central to a piece in progress. Sometimes, they provide a jolt of understanding. No, ideas don't rise like genies from a bottle. But if we rub the surface just a bit, something special can shine from within. Just as words eventually emerge from the jumble of letters on a Scrabble player's tray, string has a way of eventually sorting itself into clear and compelling patterns.

So take a few minutes several times each day to jot down observations in a notebook or on a portable electronic device. After a few weeks, reflect on the experience.

1. Has the process of gathering string made you a keener observer of your surroundings?
2. Did you notice any connections among the things you scribbled down?
3. Did the experience change the way you look at the place in which you live or work?
4. Why?
5. How?
6. Did it take you to new places, physically or in your imagination?

FIVE
THE PASSIVE OBSERVER AT WORK

Even the scenery was depressing. There was nothing to see but the snow blowing over the road and the stunted countryside rolling by in slow motion. Between Langley and Arlington even the woods looked stunted. There had been a blizzard the day before, but the landscape was all so raggedy it didn't even look good in the snow. Over the car radio he could hear John F. Kennedy delivering his inaugural address. The reception was poor, and the broadcast kept fading in and out through the static. The announcer, who spoke in hushed tones as if he were describing a tennis match, had said that it was 17 degrees in Washington and a wind was blowing on Capitol Hill and Kennedy was bareheaded and wore no overcoat.

—The Right Stuff[1]

As astronaut John Glenn drove his car past this barren snowscape, Tom Wolfe set the scene as if he were riding alongside, shotgun. Wolfe, in fact, was not there. But *Life* magazine's Loudon Wainwright was, and when Wolfe re-created this scene to start chapter 9 of his best-selling book about the first astronauts, he quite likely tapped the memories of Glenn and Wainwright alike.

Journalists build scenes in a variety of ways. Wolfe, a reporter extraordinaire who later became an acclaimed novelist, was one of a distinctive group of long-form feature writers in the 1960s who developed a genre of storytelling that became known as "new journalism." It applied the disciplined, detailed skills of depth reporting to a new kind of journalism that took its form from fiction. Wolfe and his fellow practitioners recorded or re-created events and dialogue scene by scene as if they were there as sort of ever-present observers. Sometimes, as in the case of this snowy drive, they were far away, in distance and time. But the new journalists built their stories not from imagination, as the fiction writer would, but rather from verifiable material they had accumulated through observation, documentary evidence, and in-depth interviews with those who were present.

"What interested me was not simply discovery that it is possible to write accurate non-fiction with techniques usually associated with novels and short stories," Wolfe wrote in his book *The New Journalism.* "It was that . . . it was possible . . . to excite the reader both intellectually and emotionally."[2]

In *The Right Stuff*, Wolfe took readers into Glenn's car and out to the eerie site of a test plane crash. He put readers into the cocky culture of fighter jocks and out to space. Yet, the events he wrote about had taken place years before.

Interviewing for story—not just for the facts but also for details and dialogue that set a scene and establish mood and motive—takes great skill and integrity. It requires time, patience, and exhaustive reporting. It also demands an eye and ear for the descriptive bits and pieces that establish a sense of place—things like that radio static and blowing snow that put the reader in the passenger's seat of Glenn's car.

The best way to learn what to ask about events you cannot witness is to practice describing events you *can* witness, to sort through and select the images and words that best capture them. (In chapter 9, "Interviewing for Story," we'll look at techniques for drawing telling detail from interviews.)

My advice is to start small—to record one brief encounter, one overheard conversation, or one modest exchange of everyday life. Write what you observe as a miniature story of sorts, and you'll add new shades to your writer's palette that will help color bigger works later on.

Before I send my feature-writing students out to conduct a single interview, I send them into the city of Boston, without preparation, to find and capture just such a serendipitous vignette—and to do so in less than two hundred words.

"Go someplace where you can be a fly on the wall," I instruct them. "Blend into the scenery and observe—with your eyes, your ears, your nose. You can't ask questions. You can't bring your assumptions to the page. You can't offer opinion. This is not about you. It's about what you witness." It takes a little luck, this practice of passive observation. But by locking in on life around them, keen observers make a bit of their own luck, too.

These tips can help in selecting and sketching the spontaneous scene:

1. Look for action. It shows character. Someone reading in the library doesn't make for an absorbing scene. Something needs to happen.
2. Bring your lens in tight. I'd rather watch the interplay of mother and son on the ice-skating rink than read a midrange description of what a dozen skaters there are doing.
3. Establish place. It anchors scene. Names, geographic markers, and familiar images all help.

4. Look for some kind of natural resolution. Don't invite readers into a scene and leave them hanging. In some fashion, it needs a beginning, a middle, and an end.
5. Choose each word with care. Some tell things just right.

Students find this assignment challenging, especially when they have about ninety minutes to observe, return, and write. (In the following class, I throw in a twist, telling them to shed at least forty words as they revise.)

Here is the second draft of one effort in a fall 2008 graduate class. It was written by Tripp Underwood, a rock musician turned writer.

> She sat slumped over on the bench, wrapped in an old bed sheet, a ratty bag at her feet. Her disheveled clothes and scattered possessions seemed out of place against the manicured backdrop of the Boston Public Garden.
>
> Her skin had been bronzed by the sun, which also had lightened several strands of grey in her long, dark hair, giving it the appearance of the streaks rich women dye in their $200 hair styles a few blocks away on Newbury Street.
>
> Her body rocked back and forth as she slept. Hunched over, she would abruptly right herself, only to slump forward again, as if moving to the melody of an unheard lullaby. Once she stirred, arched her head upwards, and, for a moment, parted her weathered lips in a smile, as if the warmth of the sunlight offered some comfort.

So what, you might ask, is the point? I don't give this assignment as an exercise in empty artistry. It's designed to make students sharper observers and sparer writers, to help them find details that show instead of offering opinions that tell. (You don't have to be a tuition-paying student to practice the same exercise. All you need is time, curiosity, and a notebook. A pen or pencil helps, too.)

ACTION SHOWS CHARACTER

Nonfiction writing feeds off of what people do and what those actions say about who they are. Small scenes play out in front of us every day—two teens playing speed chess in the park, a frustrated mother trying to cajole a stubborn daughter to get off the playground swings, or a frustrated driver trying to squeeze into a parking space that's just not quite big enough. Life is a collage of such snapshots. Many go unnoticed, most unrecorded. The writer who does notice these and other discrete moments begins to see stories all around (see chapter 6, "Finding Fresh Stories").

This exercise also builds writing muscles. What details show and what merely characterize? Did I choose the right verb? How do I describe a place or a person? Can I separate what I observe from what I think about it? (Underwood used verbs such as "rocked, hunched, stirred, arched, and parted" to bring action, movement, and interest to what could have been a dull description of a woman on a bench. However, he did not stray from description into opinion.)

Blogs rarely house pure observation. Readers turn to blogs in part to engage the writers, whom they expect to have views and who, at times at least, emerge as characters in their own stories. But bloggers, too, need to describe the world around them.

"If you can't write a story that has color in it, you won't be a good blogger," says John Wilpers, a former editor who, in his new business, is helping to identify the best bloggers around the world to link with traditional news organizations. "You have to use the elements of sight, sound, smell, feel."

Kathy and I returned to Aix-en-Provence in July 2010. Our last evening was Bastille Day, France's national independence day, and late that night, I posted a blog, edited a bit below, before turning in. After a two-paragraph lead, much of it simply recorded what Wilpers refers to as the "color" of the scene around us.

Aix-en-Provence, France—The only bad thing about vacations is that they eventually end. But what better grand finale than Bastille Day, France's July 4, complete with a real-life general, an oompah band, 20 minutes of fireworks set to classical music, and a disco-pop-rock orchestra accompanied by go-go girls gyrating beneath the statue of King Rene, who led Provence in the 15th century.

You really had to be there.

The official festivities began at 5 p.m. with speeches and a "parade," consisting of a few fire trucks; the general, who was driven off in a small truck he climbed into on portable steps wheeled to its side, and several dozen well-armed, marching representatives of the French military.

An upbeat, old-fashioned band, dressed in white and wearing straw hats, sat nearby, adding a bit of luster. It continued to play after the pomp and circumstance had ended—or at least tried.

By then it was 6:15 p.m. Up the street, by the statue, the evening's rock band (Orchestre XL, according to the logo on its trucks) was setting up, its horn players blasting wicked riffs through powerful amplifiers. Down the street, city workers banged around disassembling the metal gates put up for crowd control. And through the clatter and cacophony, the band played on.

"Who's in charge here?" Kathy asked.

This being the South of France, the answer seemed pretty obvious: No one discernible.

Let's put it this way. The British form neat queues and wait patiently. American lines are somewhat less orderly. In France, whether approaching a ski lift or a concert hall entrance, people form flying wedges that resolve themselves with a certain vigilant grace.

The same could be said of the clashing bands, which eventually took turns.

At 10 p.m., the fireworks began, interspersing the usual sizzles and starbursts with silent arcs of silver that intersected in the sky to a Strauss waltz. The yellow lab beside us shrank from the noisier interludes. So when the last glitter fell from the sky, his owner let him dive into one of the city's fountains in the middle of its much-photographed, tree-lined Cours Mirabeau.

And then Orchestre XL got down to business: five horns (three saxes, trumpet and trombone), five singers, bass, guitarist, synthesizer keyboardist, drummer . . . and two dancers.

First the dancers appeared in white, angel wings all aflutter through a most unusual rendition of the theme song for the musical *Mamma Mia*. Next, as the music turned to a harder-edged rock, they appeared in black leather, scooped to the waist in the back and leaving awfully little to the imagination in the front. As the light show flashed even brighter and smoke rose from the floor of the three-level stage, they re-appeared, this time almost as scantily clad as the dancers in Paris' infamous Moulin Rouge. . . .

The band's program was itself . . . eclectic. First, lots of disco ("burnin"). Then atonal rock ('90s, I think). Then the schmaltzy standby *Volare* kicked off a medley more Spanish than Italian, during which one of the dancers walked onstage dressed as a matador. Later, when the lead singer launched into a song whose chorus seemed to start with "in America," both dancers were back, this time bedecked in American flag bathing suits, caps and capes.

The French don't much like American politics. But they clearly love our culture—even if the version of it celebrated here *is* a bit dated.

—*True/Slant*

THE POWER OF ONE

At times, a single scene, observed by the writer, can serve as an iconic image, a symbol that encapsulates a much larger story. Such was the case several days and several thousand stories after Hurricane Katrina devastated New Orleans. *New York Times* reporter Dan Barry walked and drove the city's streets, starting and ending his story at the site of "The Corpse on Union Street." His piece conveyed the isolation and desolation of one of America's great cities better than anything else I read. For the most part, he merely recorded what he saw, smelled, and heard around him, a passive observer at work.

AN UNFORGETTABLE IMAGE OF KATRINA

In the downtown business district here, on a dry stretch of Union Street, past the Omni Bank automated teller machine, across from a parking garage offering "early bird" rates: a corpse. Its feet jut from a damp blue tarp. Its knees rise in rigor mortis.

Six National Guardsmen walked up to it on Tuesday afternoon and two blessed themselves with the sign of the cross. One soldier took a parting snapshot like some visiting conventioneer, and they walked away. New Orleans, September 2005.

Hours passed, the dusk of curfew crept, the body remained. A Louisiana state trooper around the corner knew all about it: murder victim, bludgeoned, one of several in that area. The police marked it with traffic cones maybe four days ago, he said, and then he joked that if you wanted to kill someone here, this was a good time.

Night came, then this morning, then noon, and another sun beat down on a dead son of the Crescent City.

That a corpse lies on Union Street may not shock; in the wake of last week's hurricane, there are surely hundreds, probably thousands. What is remarkable is that on a downtown street in a major American city, a corpse can decompose for days, like carrion, and that is acceptable.

Barry's writing is spare and specific. He shows what he sees. And he lets strong, fresh, and active verbs—jut, rise, bludgeoned, and blessed—do his work.

Sure, when it comes to pure passive observation, Barry cheats. He conducts an interview. And he ends the scene with his own observations, with the voice of the columnist he has, in fact, been. "What is remarkable is that on a downtown street in a major American city, a corpse can decompose for days, like carrion, and that is acceptable." But for the most part, in the best traditions of journalistic storytelling during catastrophes and disasters, he stands as an observer for us all.

Another reporter, Julie Sullivan, relied on pure observation in beginning the story of a trip she took with a Spokane, Washington, church group to a place thousands of miles away.

The Romanian orphanage looks abandoned. Half the roof is gone. Glass chips sprinkle the walkway. Concrete walls peel paint like old skin.

Inside is a hallway 60 yards long. The floor is slick, sticky and slick, a wetness sliding under shoes from days-old urine, fresh feces and decades of neglect. In the greenish light are children. They are naked. Their heads are shaved.

Skin gathers at their bony elbows and hangs there. A boy scratches sores that lace his body from his buttocks to his heels. So does the girl next to him. As a group of American visitors, 13 in all, enter the building, the children scream with excitement so loud that another girl covers her ears.

The orphanage staff women hurriedly pull out clothing, grabbing arms and legs, covering emaciated bottoms.

The Americans offer handfuls of bubble gum and suddenly the children are everywhere, patting pockets, pulling straps, tripping camera shutters, reaching, shrieking, yammering clamoring for something, for anything.

Only later do you realize that someone was saying, "Moma."

REVISING HELPS EVERYONE

Some years back, Sullivan, who has won national short-form feature-writing awards, told me that she struggled with this piece for the Spokane *Spokesman Review*. This lead section, 171 words, could almost stand alone as a short, passive, observational essay.

Sullivan's a far better writer than I. Still, nearly every story can be strengthened with a bit of judicious cutting. (See chapter 14, "No One Gets It Right the First Time.") That's why I force my students to do just that.

A little distance, perhaps a walk to the water cooler, can help.

In this case, for example, how much meaning would have been lost in paragraph 2 had Sullivan left out "Inside is a hallway 60 yards long" and instead gone directly to "Inside, the floor is slick, sticky and slick"? Might she have started paragraph 3 with "Skin hangs from their bony elbows?" And in paragraph 3, did she need "as a group of American visitors," or might she have recast the sentence in a way that saved a few words?

Take any paragraph I've written here, and you can probably do the same. (Hint: "here" adds little.) In tightening your own work, look first for details that slow the scene's delivery. Prime candidates are prepositional phrases—those following little words such as "of, from, by, and for."

More than three decades ago, in the precomputer age, I learned this the hard way, squirming as my editor, no. 2 pencil in hand, drew lines through what seemed like every second sentence. That editor, Rick Levine, went on to the *New York Times*. I went into academics. But his lessons—that fewer words have greater impact—stayed with me.

Before you revise, however, you have to start—by observing, writing, and reading your work aloud to a friend. If you enjoy travel, carry a small notebook when you visit places and capture vignettes as they unfold around you. (One can only hope they are less macabre than Barry's po-stapocalyptic New Orleans.)

Here's a bit from my 2007 Provence notebooks. On a beautiful long weekend in early March, Kathy and I drove south along the then-deserted French Riviera, stopping for two nights at Hotel Welcome in the tidy port village of Villefranche-sur-Mer. Warmed by the morning sun, I scribbled these lines from our second-floor balcony. All but the last few sentences are the kind of passive observation I've been encouraging you to try.

Behind Chapelle St. Pierre, which the artist Jean Cocteau painted with arched eyebrows, two eyes, and the hint of a nose, the harbor sparkles. Below, an ample, thick-haired golden retriever ambles through the town square. He passes the church, the sun-drenched, pastel-toned buildings, the couple clinking glasses at the sidewalk cafe. He walks, unhurriedly but with purpose, to the lip of the town fountain. Pausing momentarily, he plunges into its surrounding pool, splashing water onto the sidewalk in his wake. Refreshed, he stands, shakes himself, steps out, and continues on his way, his morning bath complete. We sit and watch. This is life in the slow lane: no set destination, no beating of the clock, no traffic, few people. It's what makes the South of France so special in the off season.

At the outset, practicing passive observation can work best with a partner. Each of you should construct your own vignette from the same scene. Don't consult as you write. But do share what each of you has written after the fact. First, discuss these questions together:

1. Did you notice things you might have missed had you plunged in and asked questions instead of letting the scene unfold? What?
2. What did you find most difficult about the exercise? Most rewarding?
3. What aspect of the scene was most challenging to describe—people, place, action, dialogue, or something else? Why?
4. Was it hard to keep yourself out of the story? Why?
5. Did you have to check yourself from characterizing what you saw rather than simply describing it? What is the difference?

Critique each others' work, answering these questions:

1. What do you like best about the other person's work? Why? It can be a word, a phrase, a detail, or a means of approaching or ending the scene. Start by pointing it out. Try to be specific.
2. Where, as a reader, did you stumble? Did you want to stop reading? Why? Where? (Be honest.) Does the scene confuse, jump about in time or space? Does it sink under too much detail or lack enough to hold your attention?

As a culture, we buy many more books, subscribe to many more magazines, start many more articles than we read from beginning to end. Writers can't afford to confuse or to bore, not for even a sentence. Self-indulgence can do both.

So, as you write, think crisp, concise, conversational, and compelling.

Make those the four Cs of your work, not just now but also in the future. And, oh yes, before moving to the next chapter, try revising what you've written.

SIX
FINDING FRESH STORIES

In 2008, John Wilpers set out on what some might have considered a Quixotic quest: to select the best four hundred blogs from what at the time he told me were about 114 *million* blogs worldwide.

Wilpers had convinced GlobalPost, the new international news service, that its seventy correspondents in forty-eight countries could only deliver part of the picture of the people, events, trends, and issues in each country. Top-notch bloggers, he reasoned, could round out that picture by posting about the countries from the ground up.

Wilpers's goal was to aggressively research bloggers in these countries to identify up to ten in each who blogged from a variety of perspectives, had an interesting voice, and worked in different walks of life. His aim was to have these posts published alongside the work of GlobalPost's correspondents. In return, the bloggers would not get paid but instead get global exposure, a jump in traffic, and a boost in their reputation in the field.

In his three decades in journalism, Wilpers has held nearly twenty journalism jobs, including starting five newspapers or websites from scratch. He's a risk taker. And he knew his latest quest could prove futile, profitable, or something in between. If, he reasoned, he could find enough good, knowledgeable, and passionate writers around the world, readers would hunger for their stories and perspectives on their countries.

Wilpers plan was a new twist on something editors and reporters have known for as long as journalism has been around: ordinary people can turn up extraordinary ideas for stories and have exceptional insights. As editor of the now-defunct free weekly *Boston NOW*, Wilpers had found that some can even write as well as professional reporters. During the paper's one year in existence, Wilpers put almost four thousand bloggers on his website, excerpted dozens of blog posts a day in the paper itself, and ran his news meeting online, where readers could offer suggestions in real time.

"We got some great stories from readers," he recalled. One online participant told the news meeting about a witches' coven that met every weekend on a Boston hilltop. That was a story readers couldn't resist.

Writers and publications have always relied on tips from casual acquaintances or absolute strangers to find exceptional stories. Technology, such as Wilpers's online news meetings and his collective of the "world's greatest bloggers," offers new tools for finding such "sources" as well as new outlets for citizens who want to report.

But if such tools—from the blogosphere to YouTube, Facebook, and Twitter—can complement and extend our mental faculties and physical senses, they're not designed to replace either. Curious writers will always find compelling stories by using their eyes, ears, and imagination. They notice what's changed. They recognize emerging patterns.

"The analogy I live by every day is that when astronomers look up in the sky, they see constellations," says reporter and blogger Caitlin Kelly. "They see distinct shapes that have history and context. I think great writers, great storytellers, look out in the world and see patterns. The people who are the most interesting draw connections between things."

That requires knowledge. Good writers read voraciously. Kelly says she reads all sections of the *New York Times*, the *Washington Post*, and the *Wall Street Journal* daily. She watches an hour of BBC news and surfs British, Canadian, and French newspapers online. (She also read and commented regularly on the sites of fellow bloggers at *True/Slant*.) But for all that's out there to read in the world, Kelly says, there still are many important stories not being written.

"There's so many stories that aren't being told," she says. "In any newsroom there are so many levers to push to get stories told that a lot of stories don't get told." In the blogosphere, where the only lever is the "publish" button, such obstacles disappear for storytellers willing to seek out original material. That, however, takes effort.

INVENTORYING THE OBVIOUS

A walk through an unfamiliar neighborhood can help. By letting their bodies wander in geographic space or their minds wander in cyberspace, writers can spot things in front of them so obvious that they sometimes get missed. Inventorying your own life can turn up stories as well. During my first year as an editor in California, for example, ants overran our house. On a hunch, I had a reporter check on whether others were having similar problems, and a local expert told her that an exceptionally dry year had led to an ant invasion throughout the Bay Area. The story made page 1.

Consulting sources and consulting ourselves are but two of the techniques writers use to find stories people want to read, two ways they separate themselves from the crowded field of self-publishers and the professionally published. Aware that no piece of writing can be any better than the idea at its foundation, the best storytellers devote as much time to finding original tales as they do to any other aspect of their work.

Whatever form of storytelling engages you—personal essays or profiles about others, blogging or journaling, traditional reporting or memoir—keep this in mind: if you research and write the heck out of a bad idea, you'll still have a boring story. On the other hand, if you identify or find a story that's inherently fascinating, you'll have to work to make it dull.

Sound simple? Then why are newspapers, magazines, websites, and even books filled with repetitive and predictable themes? It is, I suspect, because too many writers follow the pack, staying safely in its midst. They trail around behind the president or they chase the hot trend or hot celebrity everyone else is following, too. They add one more story to the thousands already out there on the new Supreme Court nominee or add yet one more chapter to the saga of an amateur Scottish singing sensation, Susan Boyle, whose story will likely be forgotten by the time you read these words. They bore their readers by making yesterday's news today's headlines or by simply serving up more of the same.

It is one of the reasons once-formidable newspapers in cities around the United States are on life support: no one wants to read yet more about yesterday's currency. They likely haven't for several decades, yet those stories keep coming.

"How can we make the truth as interesting to others as it is to us?" asks William Blundell, in his book *The Art and Craft of Feature Writing*. "That's the nut of it. . . . All of us share one frequently neglected responsibility: We're supposed to be tellers of tales as well as purveyors of facts. When we don't live up to that responsibility, we don't get read."[1]

Many of you, of course, have no plans to write for a traditional news outlet, yet the same advice applies. Why walk where others have already tread when you can forge a fresh path, approach your destination in a unique way? Once again, mining individual experience and intuition are the best places to start.

As the summer Olympics approached in 2008, China stood in the glare of a global spotlight. Journalists from around the world flooded Beijing. A spate of stories followed on police efforts to stop persistent problems of public spitting and the city's efforts to turn itself into a modern architectural Mecca. Such stories flowed out in the hundreds if not thousands.

Yet, the single story about China that stayed with me in the run-up to the games had nothing to do with the Olympics or the country's efforts at self-beautification. Instead, it told of one writer's experiences navigating by car in a country with poor drivers and poorer roads. Published in the *New Yorker* in November 2007, Peter Hessler's tale taught me more about China's struggles to emerge as a modern state than anything else I've read. It helped that the lesson also made me laugh out loud.

Here is how Hessler began:

> The first accident wasn't my fault. I had rented a Volkswagen Jetta and
> driven to my weekend home in Sancha, a village north of Beijing. I parked
> at the end of the road, where the pavement widens into an empty lot. It's
> impossible to drive within Sancha; like virtually all Chinese villages, it was
> built before anybody had cars, and homes are linked by narrow footpaths.
>
> About an hour after I arrived, my neighbor asked me to move the car, be-
> cause the villagers were about to mix cement in the lot. That day, Leslie, my
> wife, and I were both on our computers, trying to do some writing.
>
> "I can move it if you want," my neighbor said. His name is Wei Ziqi, and
> he had recently completed a driving course and received his license. It was
> his proudest achievement—he was one of the first in the village to learn to
> drive. I handed him the keys and sat back down at my computer. Half an
> hour later, he returned and stood in the doorway silently. I asked if every-
> thing was all right.
>
> "There's a problem with the car," he said slowly. He was smiling, but
> it was a tight Chinese grin of embarrassment, the kind of expression that
> makes your pulse quicken.
>
> "What kind of problem," I said.
>
> "I think you should come see it."
>
> In the lot, a couple of villagers were staring at the car; they were grinning,
> too. The front bumper had been knocked completely off. It lay on the road,
> leaving the Jetta's grille gaping, like a child who's lost three teeth and can't
> stop smiling. Why did everybody look so goddamn happy?
>
> "I forgot about the front end," Wei Ziqi said.
>
> "What do you mean?" I asked.
>
> "I'm not used to driving something with a front end," he said. "During my
> course, we only drove Liberation trucks. They were flat in front."

In writing this vignette, Hessler applies plenty of rules of good writing.
The six-word first sentence hooks the reader immediately, baiting the
curious and promising more mishaps to come. As he does in this opening scene, Hessler throughout the piece uses personal *anecdotes*—small
scenes from his own life—to engage readers in his bigger problem: a
country filled with bad drivers and roads that lead nowhere.

USING DIALOGUE TO PLACE THE READER

The dialogue helps establish this point and leads the reader right to
Hessler's crumpled Jetta. And his marvelous *analogy* compares the Jetta's
grille to "a child who's lost three teeth and can't stop smiling." This makes
the scene visual and familiar.

But writing skills aside (and even this veteran notes that he and his
wife "were *trying* to do some writing"), Hessler's piece works because

it frames the story of China's entry into a bumper-car culture around his own series of misadventures. He keeps his focus tight, engaging the reader in him, the writer, as well as the subject (driving in China).

Stories needn't be exotic to be interesting. They can be shaped by all kinds of ordinary experiences. During our semester in Aix-en-Provence, we lived nearly two miles from town on a one-car-wide road on which we'd begin our daily walk to town. At some point, after reading the novel *A Good Year* by author Peter Mayle, chronicler of all things Provençal, I wrote about our daily routines in an essay published by the *Christian Science Monitor*. Here is an excerpt:

> Nearly 10 weeks into our stay here, my wife, Kathy, and I are living in the slow lane, trying to measure each day by what we perceive rather than what we produce. In its way, that poses the most insurmountable challenge. For, as humorist Art Buchwald wrote in his final column, published days after his death, "What's it all about, Alfie?"
>
> For now, I'll settle for three loads of wash, drying in the breeze on a sunlit patio, hung to the unrelenting serenade of song birds in the soft light of a spring morning, with the fragrant smell of laurels for which our lane, Chemin du Vallon des Lauriers—street of the little valley of laurels—was named. (Time: about 90 minutes to hang, three days to dry.)
>
> I'll settle for throwing open the shutters each morning as the sky takes color, dodging the bees that seek *amour* on our screenless sills as I fix the latches (10 minutes).
>
> I'll settle for our daily walk to town, past the old women, wheeling carts for shopping, past the teens playing cards on the sidewalk of Lycee Paul Cezanne during a break, past the middle schoolers, jostling and giggling a few blocks farther on (45 minutes).
>
> I'll settle for Aix-en-Provence's grand Saturday morning market, as I weave through the crowds, knapsack on my back, a white shopping bag in each hand, looking for the plumpest strawberries, inhaling at tables laden with Provencal herbs, and listening to the man pounding the keys of an upright piano in the street. Relishing, too, the music of the country vendors—ruddy-faced, rough-handed—saying nothing more profound than *"voila, Merci, monsieur. Bonne journee. Au revoir."* Their music is all in the tenor and cadence of delivery of this most routine exchange of pleasantries. (Oh yes . . . time: three hours.)
>
> Life here is not so much different from the States as it is slower-paced, lived with more style and more grace. . . . Young and old, male and female, the people of Provence seem to understand the art of life and their place in it. Their eyes smile. Their hands speak. They stop and talk between food stands, forever planting light kisses on one another's cheeks (two kisses identify town people, three the country folk).
>
> As I try to perceive, to make sense of life here, sometimes my understanding falters. Words, in English and French alike, often fail me, too. I can understand why the Impressionists painted these street scenes; I can't always capture them.

Take, again, the market: the dogs curled at the feet of the vendors or carried in the handbags of shoppers. The crowded cafes, where people watch the crowds and the crowds look back. The children, waiting wide-eyed but patiently in line for their turn at the rotisserie chicken stand. The rich and succulent greens, reds, yellows and oranges of vegetables and fruits brought straight from the field. The sunlight, playing off buildings and café umbrellas. The fresh-cut flowers that cover one entire square in a blanket of color.

And, as winter turns to spring, the silly tourists, fellow Mayle fans no doubt, who try to capture the grace and charm of the South of France in a graceless moment of point-and-shoot photography.

They will fail, of course, as have I at similar moments.

Like all of life here, market day has to be lived, not transported. Halfway through our stay, this I know already. We will return in June with Provencal tablecloths, a glossy coffee-table book, hundreds of photos, posters of storefronts and, perhaps, even a decent painting.

But Provence cannot be bottled, cannot be shipped home. It has to be lived, one day at a time, doing (as Mayle writes) "so little and enjoying it so much."

Everyone's life, I'd wager, is filled with such bite-size stories. We just have to look and listen for them, to inhale life around us rather than walling ourselves off behind cell phones and iPods.

KEEPING THE SENSES ON HIGH ALERT

Using the senses can serve professional nonfiction writers just as well as the proverbial sources made famous by Deep Throat and the story of Watergate. Personal stories may not topple governments, but they do connect reader and writer in more intimate ways.

It is fresh content first, not words, that makes stories worth reading. Yet, in the world of my profession—journalism—too few reporters take time to look beyond the events announced on police blotters, wire service reports, press releases, and government agendas. They cover "buildings" instead of thematic or geographic "beats." They write about sources instead of people. They file news reports instead of personal stories, tales they might share with friends but forget to share with readers.

Whether you write for a boss or write for yourself, here, too, blogs can help, Nieman Journalism Lab director Joshua Benton says. "The question, 'Is it a story and is it interesting?' are two different questions," he told journalists at the 2008 Nieman Narrative Journalism Conference. "Blogs can shift you from the news peg model to the moment model. . . . Blogging is about capturing observations and reactions and moments at an early stage when news is both fresh and still unformed. . . . It opens up the world for a whole bunch of things that don't get into our newspapers very often."

If you wish to find such things, learn to *enterprise*, to look for the kernel of a story either off the beaten path or hidden deep within it. Here are some other ways of finding stories that tend to get overlooked.

Change Your Routines

By the third week of any class, my students have claimed seats for the semester. They never vary their pattern. We are creatures of habit. Yet, routine often dulls the senses rather than sparking them. Dare to seek a different path. Go places that pique your curiosity. Watch a baseball game from the bleachers. Dawdle awhile in the public park to listen to that street musician, to observe. Visit an emergency room, late at night, in a tough part of town.

One of my favorite reporters, now a columnist for the *San Jose Mercury News*, relished the wandering days I'd give reporters as enticements to break the patterns of their work. As he drove around, he saw a used book cart standing unattended near the San Jose State University campus and wrote about its proprietor, who built his living on the trust of those who'd take a book and leave a quarter. He knocked on the door of a former Nebraska farmer whose lawn was cluttered with miniature windmills and asked what so many others who'd driven past must have wanted to ask: "How come?" He watched as a Vietnamese specialty food store opened its doors next to a Mexican American counterpart and discovered the owners were collaborating rather than competing.

When the San Jose airport expanded, forcing a neighborhood to relocate, that reporter, Mike Cassidy, stopped by to chat with the last family to move on. His piece began like this:

> Let's just say they don't have many block parties down on Anita Street, where John Pena and his two children live.
> See, the Penas are the block. In fact, they're the whole neighborhood—or what's left of it.
>
> —*San Jose Mercury News*

Look for Stories beyond and behind the Events Called News

Every newspaper is a repository of tips to stories waiting to be told. The *Boston Globe*'s September 10, 2008, edition was no exception.

On that day, the Massachusetts Port Authority unveiled a four-million-dollar glass and steel memorial named "A Place of Remembrance" at Boston's Logan Airport, a shrine of sorts to the 147 passengers and crew members killed September 11, 2001, on United Flight 175 and American Airlines Flight 11, which originated at Logan.

The memorial's unveiling drew dignitaries such as Massachusetts governor Deval Patrick, and it resulted in predictable news coverage. The *Globe* wrote about the memorial, its structure, and its cost. The story included a moving quote or two from victims' families and a picture of the event. What was missing were the personal stories, those that looked at the memorial not as a structure but rather as a memory of loved ones lost.

News events, whether marking the unveiling of a memorial, the awarding of a medal, or the presentation of an honorary degree, too often miss the emotion and meaning of the moment. These can best be conveyed by "bringing the lens in tight," telling individual stories about those who are touched by or who played a special part in making concept reality. Such tales, the storyteller's domain—sometimes called "features off the news" by journalists—convey the impact of news in ways facts alone cannot.

What kinds of stories? In this case, I'd have liked to spend the day beside a relative or loved one visiting the memorial for the first time. Was this day just one more prick of pain or, in some way, did it help healing? I would have liked to read about the man or woman who fought to build this memorial and perhaps overcame early resistance. I'd have liked to hear how the final design came to be. And I'd have liked a more intimate glimpse of those who gathered on this first day and why they came.

News reports give the facts but don't always convey understanding. Each of these stories "off the news" of the unveiling might have contributed to readers' understanding by giving those readers a *place to stand* to witness events.

Look for Those Affected

Statistics can convey the scope of damage in an earthquake, the number of those without health care, and the breadth of job loss in a recession. But they don't capture sacrifice, suffering, or perseverance. Stories that do almost always talk about the struggle of one neighborhood to rebuild, the obstacles faced by one couple confronting failing health, and the saga of one unemployed worker seeking to rebuild her life. News often summarizes government reports. Stories make them human. They give the news a "face" by showing its impact on individuals.

For all the thousands of stories churned out about the global downturn, it was those like a *New York Times* series titled "Living with Less: The Human Side of Global Recession" that made it seem real. Here is how one installment began:

> Lincoln, Calif.—The Ferrells have cut back on dance lessons for their twin daughters. Vaccinations for the family's two cats and two dogs are out. Haircuts have become a luxury.

And before heading out recently to the discount grocery store that has become the family's new lifeline, Sharon Ferrell checked her bank account balance one more time, dialing the toll-free number from memory.

"Your available balance for withdrawal is $490.40," the disembodied electronic voice informed her.

At the store with that number firmly in mind, she punched the price of each item into a calculator as she dropped it into her cart, making sure she stayed under her limit. It was all part of a new regimen of fiscal restraint for the Ferrells, begun in January, when state workers, including Mrs. Ferrell's husband, Jeff, were forced to accept two-day-a-month furloughs.

For millions of families, this is the recession: not a layoff, or a drastic reduction in income, but a pay cut that has forced them to thrash through daily calculations similar to the Ferrells'. Even if workers have managed to avoid being laid off, many employers have cut back in other ways, reducing employees' hours, imposing furloughs and even sometimes trimming salaries.

—*New York Times*

Tell stories of how events affect ordinary lives. Most of us—your potential readers—live them.

Ask Yourself "Why?"

During his days as a reporter for the *Baltimore Sun*, Jon Franklin won two Pulitzer Prizes, journalism's highest honor. Later, he taught journalism and wrote an excellent book, *Writing for Story*, that annotated two of his stories in making a case for more dramatic narrative nonfiction writing in journalism.

To Franklin, great stories are often hidden in the "briefs," the few paragraph-long tidbits that tell of a prize, an honor, or an award, but never look behind it to examine what the individual overcame to get to this point. He writes, "Most news stories are endings with no beginning attached."[2]

The writer who finds those beginnings—and chronicles the obstacles people overcome to reach the endings—gets the best story. It might delve into why an eighty-five-year-old crossed the stage to accept that college degree she's finished after a sixty-year hiatus; why the paraplegic climber decided to scale rock faces; or why the foster family, honored for raising two dozen children, took in its first.

Asking the question "why" can also establish motives that are less honorable. Here's how writer Michael Crowley began an article in *Rolling Stone* that looked at why so many in Congress, Democrats included, wanted to raise from seven to ten million dollars the amount protected from inheritance tax.

On a recent April day in Barack Obama's America, where equality is on the rise and greed is on the run, a Democratic senator from an impoverished Southern state took a brave stand—on behalf of the country's richest families.

On April 1st, Sen. Blanche Lincoln of Arkansas, a state with the nation's third-lowest medium income, sponsored a budget amendment that would sharply reduce taxes on the estates of millionaires after they die.

—*Rolling Stone*

Measure Change

In 1968, Americans shuddered as first Martin Luther King then Robert Kennedy were gunned down. Forty years later, the Democratic Party nominated a tall black man with an unusual name to be president of the United States. His sweeping victory in the subsequent election realigned political party coalitions in ways that could prove lasting or might merely be ephemeral.

Though it can get lost in the rough-and-tumble realities of daily life, change—sometimes subtle, sometimes gut wrenching—is a predictable component of community and society, not merely a compelling campaign slogan. That change can also be a powerful source of stories.

Sometimes there's no marker for change other than the observer's sharp eye. The abandonment of our agrarian Midwest can be seen in the shuttered stores and barnyards of small towns as well as measured in the declining number of family farms and the shrinking census counts in these communities.

A few years ago, the *New York Times* looked at this phenomenon in a series called "Vanishing Point." One of these stories, by Timothy Egan, measured this long, slow decline as the context for a story about one community's effort to save its school—and stay alive.

Superior, Neb.—When death comes to a small town, the school is usually the last thing to go. A place can lose its bank, its tavern, its grocery store, its shoe shop. But when the school closes, you might as well put a fork in it.

So it was in Hardy, one of many last-gasp towns in Nuckolls County, Neb., along the Kansas state line. A rock memorial, overgrown by grass and weeds, rests like a tombstone under sagging football goal posts. The stone marks where the Hardy school used to be, where the wind carried voices of children—the joyous static of tomorrow.

This year, Nuckolls County, population 4,843, lost another two schools, to budget cuts and declining enrollment, perhaps dooming another pair of towns to Hardy's fate in a region that has seen nearly two-thirds of its population disappear since 1920.

But here in Superior, whose slogan is "An oasis of the Great Plains, in the middle of everywhere," and which claims to be the exact same distance from Los Angeles and New York, they have made a last stand.

Sometimes writers can measure change simply by marking their calendars. Historic dates provide a rationale—a *news peg*—for writing stories that look at what's different or new, at how things have changed. Writer David Filipov used one such anniversary, September 11, 2008, to tell a deeply personal story, "Trying to Move On," which, by his own acknowledgment, he had evaded for seven years. It began like this:

> **New York**—Seven years ago today, terrorists flew the plane carrying my father into the World Trade Center.
>
> The crash of American Airlines Flight 11 was an extraordinarily public event. The death of the man who gave me my passion for sailing, baseball, playing the guitar, and telling a story is my private tragedy. I've never wanted to mix the two, the public with the private.
>
> Everyone has seen the grainy video of the Boeing 767 slamming into the North Tower and exploding into flames. I've seen it far too many times. Every Sept. 11, countless memorial services, blood drives, and charity events commemorate the day. I've never been to any of them. Tens of thousands have paid their respects at ground zero. I had never been able to bring myself to come here.
>
> Until now.
>
> As a son, I decided it was time to finally visit the place where my father died, and try to move on. And what I saw is that ground zero has moved on too.
>
> In some ways, the locus of one of America's greatest tragedies has become just another storied block in this storied city, as normal as the passenger planes that descend over the Manhattan skyline on a clear September morning like silver dragonflies.
>
> —*Boston Globe*

Whether it measures the subtlety of an evolving rural landscape or the starkness of one of America's most painful anniversaries, change is as constant as the passage of time. Ask yourself, "How have things changed and who felt that change most keenly?" The answers will likely lead toward an interesting story.

Challenge Your Comfort Zone

Sit down and draw up a list of all the people and places your local newspaper or hyperlocal website does not cover regularly or well. Are the aging in your community invisible? How about the disabled, the poor, the unemployed, or underemployed? If the first step in finding stories is to take stock of what's not been covered, the second is to figure out what should be. Sometimes that means pushing yourself past your personal comfort zone.

As more and more of those running and writing for American news outlets are drawn from better-educated and better-heeled backgrounds, more and more of America's less privileged are simply being ignored. The gaps of coverage got bad enough in South Florida in the early 1990s that the Poynter Institute for Media Studies in St. Petersburg invited two reporters from each local newspaper and television station to take monthly field trips to such "ethnic" places as a funeral home in the black community and an outdoor marketplace in a neighborhood of Asian immigrants.

It doesn't take a grant to go someplace that may be unfamiliar, just a fresh eye, a willingness to listen, and perhaps a little introspection into our own biases.

Look for Patterns

Garden-variety crimes are the stuff of four-inch "briefs" and filler in daily newspapers. But sometimes a pattern of crimes—such as a Boston bank robber who created diversions by setting off bomb scares before each daring daytime bank robbery—makes for a compelling read.

Here, a *Wall Street Journal* reporter noted a new pattern in the way police are fighting crime:

> When a burglar broke into a home on the outskirts of Riverdale Park, Md., last month, some locals quickly received an email alert about the incident. Once police confirmed the crime on the scene, they followed up with a more thorough email disclosing the time, location and type of crime.
>
> The alert is part of a crime-information service that the Riverdale Park police department provides its residents about illegal activity in their neighborhoods. "It helps us keep the public informed," says Teresa Chambers, police chief of Riverdale Park, a suburb of Washington, D.C. "It's also a way for us to solicit help [from residents] in solving some of these crimes."
>
> Across the country, Americans can increasingly track crime trends block by block as more police departments contract with Internet-based crime-mapping services. Since 2007, more than 800 police departments have begun working with Web sites like CrimeMapping.com, CrimeReports.com and EveryBlock.com. The services take live feeds from police record-keeping systems and automatically post the data on their sites.

Sometimes patterns are evident in the day-to-day annoyances of life. Who, for example, hasn't been frustrated by the mounting maze of programmed phone menus seemingly intent on freezing angry or frustrated consumers out? Who hasn't been besieged by the exponential growth of programmed calls, intent on catching those same consumers in?

Though pattern or trend stories take measure of a broader, unannounced phenomenon in news or culture, they often do so by using one or more central characters to illustrate it. A few years ago, for example, I wrote a story for *Westchester* magazine about a new brand of cyberspace gunslingers— the cocky, computer-savvy players in the growing world of online poker.

I built the story around one college student rapidly on the path of making the game his means of making a living. Here is how it began.

> He's 20 years old, quirky, quick and plenty bright: Ivy League, a perfect 800 on his Math SAT's. But No-Man as we'll call him, didn't spend this summer interning on Wall Street or networking in New York's financial corridors. Heck, he barely got out of his pajama bottoms and T shirt at his parent's Ossining home.
>
> Like others in a growing army of college kids in Westchester and across the country, he spent his summer staring at his computer into the wee hours, betting hundreds of dollars each night in the fast-paced, silent and instantly available world of online poker.

Some pattern stories are merely "trendy"—the hippie communes of the sixties come to mind as do any number of consumer culture phenomena from Cabbage Patch dolls to, well, online poker.

Other patterns illuminate a path of serious change in local, regional, or national life. Today, for example, my contemporaries—fifty- and sixty-something boomers—are selling their suburban homes and moving into cities, changing the economies and culture of both. And if their rural communes were once merely trendy, many of the kids who moved to the country in states like Vermont in the sixties stayed, made middle-class homes there, and today serve as the pillars of their local communities.

New waves of immigrants—Mexican, Russian, and Haitian, to name a few—are creating patterns of migration today that present stories waiting to be written.

Spotting patterns before everyone else takes confidence and sometimes help. I'd suggest setting up weekly brainstorming sessions with a few friends, online or over coffee. Ask yourselves these questions:

1. What's new?
2. What's different?
3. What's changed?
4. Who in your community do you never read about?
5. What neighborhoods, stores, organizations, or places in your community would you like to learn more about? Why?
6. What are your friends, kids, parents, or co-workers talking about?

Find the answers to these questions, and a story awaits.

Try this exercise as well. Get a good set of maps to your community. Once each week walk a part of it that you've never visited before. Chat with people mowing their lawns or walking dogs. Stop in local coffee shops, barber shops, and beauty shops. Ask the people there what's new in their lives and their neighborhood, what they believe the media are neglecting to cover, what concerns them, and what they're excited about.

Their answers could surprise you. Remember, storytelling always starts with discovery, both about our own lives and the lives of others.

SEVEN
RECONNAISSANCE

Fresh out of graduate school, I set out in my first month as a reporter at the (Bergen County) *Record* to gather information about a Ridgewood, New Jersey, dispute involving a group home for troubled teenage girls. Ridgewood was one of two sleepy, affluent suburban communities I'd been assigned to cover as my first *beat*, the geographic area I was supposed to comb for news and feature stories.

As I knocked on the door of that home, I recall having next to no idea what story I intended to tell. I knew that someone at a village council meeting had told me the home was controversial. Neighbors didn't want it there; they didn't like the idea of living near a house occupied by teens who had faced difficulties with their families, schools, and, in some cases perhaps, the courts. My editor suggested I check things out. But he didn't suggest how I should approach the story. New to my job, I didn't dare ask.

Looking back after all these years, I suspect the story could have been interesting. The home's director allowed me to talk to the girls without staff present. The neighbors' concerns could well have had at least some merit; this was an upscale place, and some of these kids might have been in trouble. Regardless, the story was steeped in the kind of conflict of class, property, and personality that makes for rich reading.

As I pulled pad from pocket, I might have asked questions aimed at fleshing out the conflict between the home and its neighbors. Was it a classic case of NIMBYism (not in my backyard) in affluent, suburban America, or something else? Or I might have explored whether any of the girls had gotten to know a neighbor or had overcome the stereotype and stigma of the "troubled teen" and engaged in some other way in the community. Had I looked, perhaps I might have found an even better story, that of a girl who had found the help and encouragement in home and community to "graduate" and move on.

I might have. But instead I wrote . . . nothing.

Back then, green and nervous, none of this was obvious to me, in large part because I had failed, as reporters like to say, to *do my homework* before knocking on the door that day. I knew little about the home, who lived there, or why. I knew even less about the neighbors' concerns. So when I arrived at about 10:00 a.m. with a notebook, a tape recorder, and a slew of old-fashioned magnetic tapes, I just let the girls ramble. I left late that afternoon with hours of interviews from the home's residents, who had regaled me with their sad stories, delighted, no doubt, to be able to bend the ear of an earnest young male reporter for an entire day. What I didn't have was a story. I'd listened attentively but let them lead me wherever they wanted. And I left as clueless about what I might write as I had arrived.

This was not my only bad day during my early months reporting in Bergen County. I squeaked through my three-month probation, working sixty-five- and seventy-five-hour weeks, doing all but shut out the lights as I dragged myself home regularly at two and three in the morning. I wrote lots of basic news stories—about new fire stations, a toxic spill that poisoned ducks at the local pond, and the exciting news that Ridgewood had changed insurance carriers. These news reports papered the inside pages of the *Record*'s B-section, earnest little pieces that perhaps satisfied community officials and those who follow every bend and turn of community affairs, but likely no one else.

My problems as reporter and writer back then were multiple. The biggest, however, was that I hadn't grasped the steps needed to define a story's direction and form. First, I rarely took the time to think: "What is my story, and why should readers care?" No two questions are more important for a writer starting out on a project. (See chapter 1, "Finding a Place—and Space—to Think.")

Yet, even if I had stopped to reflect, I would likely have remained in the dark, because often I had not done the preliminary background work— the *reconnaissance*—I needed to figure out the answer.

ESTABLISH THE STORY'S BLUEPRINT EARLY

Good reporters, good researchers, try to define a story's boundaries early. Like surveyors, they plot a perimeter. Like architects, they think out the scale, design, and form of what they're building—and not merely before they start writing but also before they do their most intense research. The parallel is simple: no architect in his or her right mind would instruct a contractor to buy doorknobs, window frames, beams, flooring, and roofing without a clear sense of a house's size and design. And no writer wants to gather together all of his or her building materials—the facts, details, quotes, and anecdotes around which stories are constructed— without knowing the story's scope and shape. For both, working without a blueprint is a waste of time.

"Think small," suggests William Zinsser in *On Writing Well*. "Decide what corner of your subject you're going to bite off, and be content to cover it well."[1]

Identifying and reducing the scale of a writing project begins with the title of this chapter: reconnaissance. Had I done some reconnaissance, for example, I would have known the nature of residents' complaints from Ridgewood Village Council minutes, from letters sent to the village clerk, and by interviewing those who lived nearby. I could have read the annual reports, brochures, and mission statements of the organization running the group home so that I understood its goals, who was eligible to stay there, and how the residents spent their days. Did some of the girls have jobs? Was it a goal for them to contribute to the community? I had no idea. I also might have stopped by the local police station to see if any complaints had been filed against the home or the girls who lived there. Such background reporting unearths details—names, facts, anecdotes, and other information, that build story. More importantly, it helps set a story's course, its focus.

After writers understand the dimensions and direction of a story, they can boil their version of that architect's blueprint down to a succinct sentence or short paragraph, a focus statement (see chapter 8, "Honing the Focus"). These, unlike the foundations of homes, are not cast in concrete; words need no hammer claw or bulldozer to dismantle. Still, writers approach these blueprints carefully and purposefully. They know that spending a little time digging the right foundation for a story can prevent the writer from wasting hours trying to build off of no foundation at all.

"The good writers I know always do some kind of planning before they report and again before they write," notes William Blundell in his book *The Art and Craft of Feature Writing*.[2]

GOOGLE ISN'T THE ONLY ANSWER

In this Internet age, too many young writers mistakenly believe that reconnaissance begins and ends with a Google search. In the 1970s, there was no Internet. But today, had I typed in "group homes" and "Northern New Jersey," I would have come up with 12,700 "hits," most of them irrelevant. An advanced Google search can sometimes unearth more helpful information. But there are many more targeted sources to search.

Take my feature article about the game *pétanque*, or boules, and its place in Provençal culture. I sold it to "Back Story," a back page feature of the *Christian Science Monitor*, before I knew much about the topic. I'd seen the game played in every town square. I'd read funny accounts of it in the books of Peter Mayle. I'd played once or twice with fellow students in my French-language immersion classes. But to really establish a focus, a way of approaching the piece—particularly in a country where my language skills could barely get me to the nearest WC—I needed to find out much more.

I did several things. On an advanced Google search I typed "history of pétanque." That led me to 207 English-language sites, including one promisingly titled "Pétanque links." Here, I found a history of the game and discovered its name came from two Provençal words that meant "feet fixed." I learned that variations of the game dated back to ancient times and that the modern version was first played in the Mediterranean village of La Ciotat, less than an hour from our Provençal apartment. I also discovered that the largest manufacturer of pétanque gear had opened a small museum near the French Riviera in the village of Vallauris.

(There, I soon confirmed my hunch that pétanque is not merely a game in the South of France. It is a central part of Provençal culture.)

LEXIS-NEXIS PROVIDES JOURNALISTIC BACKGROUND

I was off to a good start, but I needed more: someone, for starters, whom I could interview in English. First, I culled articles in U.S. newspapers, using the LexisNexis database subscribed to by my college and most libraries. By reviewing what professional journalists have already written on a subject, a writer can get a sense of what's been "covered," or told, and what's been overlooked. I was also looking for a leading figure in the field I might approach as a guide—an expert who could point me toward potential sources and give me a big-picture overview of the game's development. Then I put out an inquiry on www.profnet.com, which describes itself as "an online community of nearly 14,000 professional communicators . . . created in 1992 to connect reporters easily and quickly with expert sources."

LexisNexis led me to an article by humorist Dave Barry about one Philippe Boets, a Flemish Belgian who had begun Pétanque America to promote the game from his home somewhere in the Carolinas.

I couldn't visit, always my preference. But I could talk to him—in a language I could actually speak. Once I tracked him down, Boets proved a font of information and connections, the guide for whom I was looking. Though he didn't appear in my article, he interceded to set up an interview with Mayle, the author, and steered me to an intense, young Yale University law professor who spends his summers playing pétanque competitively in Provence.

My query on Profnet—a request to talk with some of the site's self-identified experts on the game—proved even more profitable. One response to my query came from Mitzi Gimenez, then president of San Diego's pétanque club. Her husband, Alain Gimenez, is a Frenchman, and, best of all, the couple planned to return to Marseilles, France, that summer to compete in the biggest annual pétanque competition in the world. Mitzi would become the first woman to compete as part of a team in the men's division. And the couple was to be joined on the team by Alain's father, a retired Marseilles cop named Jean-Pierre.

My reconnaissance was complete:

- I'd learned of the game's history, rules, and role, and, better yet, affirmed my hunch that it held a particular place in not only in the country's culture of sports but also in its culture of argumentation. This would become my article's focus (see chapter 8, "Honing the Focus").
- I'd identified important characters, a family that would give me the means to make the story human and personal, a way to illustrate the game's cultural role.
- I'd even found something of a *news peg*, that they were practicing to take their place in the biggest annual event of the sport worldwide.

Unlike thirty years earlier, I had found the story when it hit me between the eyes. And so, before I headed out to interview Jean-Pierre, the retired cop who speaks no English, I could assure my editor that the story was on track. I knew I'd have something worth writing, even if words in his language failed me.

As always on my forays interviewing in French, Kathy came along, both to help with translation and because—well—let's just say that Frenchmen aren't yet entirely liberated and she's a lot more attractive than I. We arrived on a day that Jean-Pierre's washing machine had overflowed. His cousin had died the night before. But neither event kept him from taking us to his beloved pétanque club. The visit provided the ending to the article, whose lead is in chapter 1.

Jean-Pierre insists his fellow club members are behind his (co-ed tournament) team, though the all-male contingent at the club the day I visit suggests liberation has yet to arrive. I've come to watch Jean-Pierre, a retired cop who plays at least two hours a day. But soon I'm playing against him, trying mightily not to embarrass myself too badly.

Jean-Pierre's team has the game's talker, a tall fellow in a white straw hat who seems determined to keep me on my heels.

"So what's the allowed diameter of each boule [pétanque ball]?" he asks.

I haven't a clue.

"65 to 80 millimeters," he says.

"How far do you throw the cochonnet [the target]?"

"Six to 10 meters?"

"That's right."

Later as his teammate shoots, he snaps a command at me. "Two meters. Two meters."

That, I learn, is how much breathing room the competition is supposed to give the shooter to keep from distracting him. ("Supposed to" is the operative phrase here.)

Later, as I prepare to shoot, I get my revenge. "Two meters. Two meters," I tell him.

"*Bien*," he says, nodding in approval. He stops jabbering and backs off.

I'm not sure I contributed much to my team's 2-games-to-1 victory that day. But I know I scored at least one point—a beginner's parry in the art of argumentation.

—*Christian Science Monitor*

LET THE TOPIC DICTATE YOUR RECONNAISSANCE

Be forewarned. There's no catch-all list of places to go for a story's reconnaissance (also called *backgrounding*). The nature of the topic dictates some of your stops. A story on the relationship between two immigrant groups in a changing neighborhood might call for data from the U.S. Census Bureau as well as interviews with organizations helping with resettlement. One on the impact of underemployment during a recession will likely include data from state and federal bureaus that gather labor statistics and a stop by retraining and unemployment centers.

One great compilation of research sites can be found at the home page of Sree Sreenivasan (www.sree.net/), dean of students at Columbia University's School of Journalism and an international lecturer on Web research. His link to "Smarter Surfing: Better Use of Your Web Time" offers a wealth of links to source guides, facts, specialized information, and resources, broad and specific.

If, for example, you're contemplating a story about Tunisia's efforts to lure scantily clad tourists to its traditional and tightly controlled shores, the CIA World Factbook might be a good jumping-off point. It will tell you 98 percent of the country's ten million people are Muslim and that President Zine el Abidine Ben Ali, who took power in a bloodless coup, has "sought to defuse rising pressure for a more open society."

If you're seeking adequate background to focus a story on a new procedure for open heart surgery, either www.webmd.com or www.mayoclinic.com might help.

The data, of course, is just a start. It gives vital context to a story, pinpoints some of the statistics that give a piece authority. But often the toughest part of reconnaissance is finding the right main subject—the individual whose personal experience universalizes the experience of others. That requires reporting at street level. "This territory can be tough on strangers, but we have to go there to gather details and direct experiences that *show* the reader," William Blundell writes in *The Art and Craft of Feature Writing*.[3]

When Dirk Johnson wrote a profile of a woman who couldn't stop smoking for the *New York Times*, he drew its street-level power from his main character, Jan Binder, a woman whose story gave new insight into a topic that otherwise might have been seen as dated and mundane. Here is an excerpt:

Sycamore, Ill.—There are few riddles in life more enigmatic than the spell that smoking can cast, even to smokers like Jan Binder, a smart 38-year-old who has walked the horror chamber of nicotine.

It was two years ago, sitting in a hospital room, that a doctor looked into the eyes of her husband, James, and told him, "Mr. Binder, you have lung cancer."

That evening her husband walked through the door at home, switched on a lamp, turned to her and sized up his life.

"I don't regret anything," he told her, "except a few million cigarettes."

Seven months later, he was dead. He was 37. Their daughter Mary was 7 years old. Kate was 5.

"When they told Jim he was going to die," Ms. Binder said, "and I saw the look on his face, I knew I would never smoke again."

She was certain sheer willpower could do it. But it was like willing herself to stop drawing breath.

She has tried going cold turkey. She has tried the nicotine patch. She has tried the drug Zyban.

Nothing has worked for more than a week.

—*New York Times*

Reconnaissance frames a story's front door. It turns a hazy idea into a focused concept; it moves the writer from generality to a specific approach. It gives the writer a path to follow rather than leaving the writer to bushwhack through brambles.

And it takes practice. Start with this exercise:

1. Brainstorm two or three topics that interest you.
2. Research what has been written about them.
3. Ask yourself what questions your research has raised.
   - Did you notice any corner of past stories that needs more development?
   - Did some aspect of the story intrigue you?
   - Was a particular perspective or viewpoint left out?
4. What stories did the answers to these questions suggest?
5. What approach might these stories take? Why?
6. What are your next steps?

Write a short memo, a few paragraphs long, outlining how you might narrow the broader topic to a specific story angle or approach.

EIGHT
HONING THE FOCUS

A strong storyline needs to be concise, arousing, and expressible in a
sentence or two.

—Writing as Craft and Magic[1]

That advice, by author Carl Sessions Stepp, is worth reading again,
this time out loud. Every story needs a story line, a single dominant
reason for being written—and read. With most stories, the best time
to establish that story line is not when you sit down to write, stacks
of disjointed notes piled around you. Instead, it is immediately after
you've completed your initial reconnaissance or background—early
enough, in other words, to inform the rest of your reporting as well as
your writing.

What Stepp calls that "expressible sentence or two" has another name.
It is called a *focus statement or theme statement*. It may sound a bit book-
ish, but it's also essential. A focus statement sets the story's direction,
implicitly dictating what information the reporter will need to gather to
write the story well.

After Hurricane Katrina battered New Orleans, for example, no reporter wandering around Louisiana would have gotten very far looking
for a story on "the aftermath." That's sort of like going to Mumbai to write
about "the city" or going to Afghanistan to write about "the war." The
scope of such approaches is so broad and so vast that a reporter looking
to research such a story would end up paralyzed.

In Louisiana, thousands of stories, each with a different focus, waited
to be told. There were stories about acts of heroism and cowardice, about
why and how New Orleans levees had failed and where the devastation
had been most intense, about programs to support residents crippled by
the storm, and about scam artists that were trying to rip them off. Reporters looking to write about "the aftermath" had to identify and then
narrow their focus—story by story—to uncover different corners of the
disaster.

Some stories weren't about New Orleans at all. At one point, for example, the *Los Angeles Times* sent a reporter to measure the impact of those streaming from New Orleans to the state's capital, Baton Rouge. The writer assigned that story might, after some preliminary calls, have sat down to craft a focus statement to set the direction and sell editors on the piece.

Perhaps it might have read something like this:

> **Boomtown**—In Katrina's aftermath, the Louisiana capital of Baton Rouge has become a boomtown. Hotels are packed, apartment rents are soaring and homes that have sat on the market for months are being snapped up at more than market price. A look at the hurricane's impact on Louisiana's capital.

With such a focus statement in place, a reporter setting to work on this story would have known where to look and what to ignore. The reporter would, for instance, have looked for personal stories that could show how Baton Rouge had become a boomtown and interviewed some of the colorful and crestfallen characters who had moved there from New Orleans. The reporter would have looked for people who had profited and perhaps some who had gouged. And in addition to the "people sources," the reporter would look for data, measuring hotel occupancy rates, changes in food and furniture prices, and increases in rents and housing costs—a range of facts that would have developed and *supported* the focus statement's assertion.

By the same token, the reporter would not have spent any time visiting New Orleans or talking to police or emergency services people there, unless those agencies had helped resettle residents in Baton Rouge.

A STRONG FOCUS ENABLES DEEPER REPORTING

What to research, and what to report, always involves choice. Focus statements help writers make those choices while they are still in the field, enabling them to go deeper into a topic rather than skimming a broad surface.

Each fall, my colleague and I ask our introductory graduate students to find out what's new in our lives and to write a focus statement that could be used as a roadmap for a *profile*, a story about us for an Emerson College student newspaper. The "what's new" part, we tell them, can help sort out what's changed and why. It gives them a chance to find something that's timely, an element of good journalism that can make a story more compelling. (From time to time, for example, stories are written about individuals released after years in prison because they were wrongly convicted. A writer looking to cover the broader issue would want to focus on someone recently released, not someone freed a decade ago.)

The task for students assigned to research me isn't easy; my life doesn't scream for coverage. Knowing their audience is the college paper helps (writers always need to be cognizant of their audience). Looking at not only what's new in my life but also what those facts say about my motivation can help, too (profiles typically want to give insights into what makes someone "tick").

First, I suggest that students simply list what's new. For 2009, that list might have been culled to this:

1. I turned sixty.
2. I got a new puppy (my third golden retriever).
3. I climbed a mountain, albeit a small one, for the first time since failing to make it up Switzerland's Matterhorn four years earlier.
4. I went to Montreal JazzFest.
5. I started a new blog for *True/Slant*.
6. I missed another deadline on this book about writer's block, though I was getting closer to finishing.
7. I had just concluded an academic year in which I was awarded the college's teaching prize.

The next challenge, I tell students, is to synthesize and analyze the key facts to determine whether any patterns or contradictions develop. Can any of these seemingly disparate facts be joined in a coherent thread?

From our discussion, the following possible focus points emerged:

1. A story about a blocked writer who teaches writing for a living.
2. A story about a man who keeps banging into obstacles (i.e., mountains and writing) even when rebuffed the first time around.
3. A story about a veteran writer—it sounds so much better than old—still struggling to unlock the secret of what blocks him.

Choosing one approach helps define future reporting; it establishes a story line. Let me take a stab:

> **Lanson**—As he starts his twenty-sixth year as a teacher of writing, Jerry Lanson still struggles with his own writing demons. He's the first to tell you that he finds deadlines daunting and rigorous routines tough to sustain. But Lanson keeps teaching, perhaps because, as he tells his students, he's struggled to overcome just about everything they're going to face. A profile.

Again, the focus statement dictates a certain direction to the reporting. This writer clearly would have wanted to establish background by looking at the drafted pages of this book. The writer would have wanted to talk to those intimately familiar with my obstacles in writing it (my wife comes to mind) and frustrated by them (my publisher comes to mind). The writer would also have wanted to talk to my colleagues and former students, to observe me in the classroom, and to compare what I say in the classroom and sometimes fail to do at the keyboard. (This writer might have wanted to interview former editors as well.)

The focus statement, however, also limits where the writer would need to look. That I love my dog and granddaughter (not in that order) is irrelevant to this story. That I like reading about politics or that I attended Haverford College and the University of Missouri are irrelevant, too—unless something I was taught in those places scarred my writing process.

Every good focus statement, in short, maps the nature and breadth of research and reporting that will follow it. This is not to suggest that reporters are ever handcuffed by fifty or so words typed on a page. Stories, like roads, sometimes change. Perhaps your original map missed the new highway. Or maybe a forest fire forced a diversion. Stories must also take unusual turns. Research uncovers something more interesting. Original assumptions prove wrong. Then writers reprogram their internal Global Positioning System (GPS); they recalibrate their story's focus or direction.

But just because roadwork can cause a detour doesn't mean we head out of state with no map or GPS. We need something to guide our trip. For writers, that GPS is a focus statement. It guides their stories.

SCUFFLING WITH A FOGGY FOCUS

Recently, I forgot this advice once again and paid the price. What started haphazardly as a quick blog evolved into a column on the future of newspapers. What started as a thirty-minute riff ended as a three-day ordeal, complete with four revisions (see chapter 14, "No One Gets It Right the First Time").

I know exactly what went wrong: I didn't focus up front, writing a few sentences that encapsulated my point. Instead, I tried to figure it out by dumping more than one thousand words onto my computer screen. Bad idea.

In retrospect, the focus I forgot to find was simple enough. (In retrospect, it usually is.) It might have gone something like this:

> **Newsroots**—Newspapers can help reclaim their audiences by returning to their populist roots. They should unearth fresh news in their community's cafés and civic centers instead of echoing today's digital and electronic media on tomorrow's front pages. Here's how.

I'll bet if I'd written those sentences as I set out, I'd have needed but two drafts. (I never get things right the first time.) Figuring out those few sentences—in other words, establishing a clear theme—would have saved at least several hours of work.

Why? Because those sentences, as in any focus statement, would have served several purposes.

1. They would have framed the story.
2. They would have set its course. I'm not just writing about "newspapers," an enormously broad topic. I am writing about how to *save* newspapers.
3. They would have helped "sell" the story by being a bit provocative.
4. They would have set its tone and approach.

Sometimes focus statements have a fifth purpose. They establish the *news peg*, the event, report, or trend that leads the writer to take on the topic. When I finally unraveled the spool of string obscuring my story's core, I sold it to the *Christian Science Monitor* by framing the story around the news peg of an ongoing union dispute at the *Boston Globe*. It began like this:

> **Boston**—The *Boston Globe* moved a step closer to the brink last night when its editorial union rejected what amounts to a 10 percent wage cut, leading management to follow up on its threat to slash pay even more.
>
> Conventional wisdom holds that newspapers have been crippled by the flight of advertising to the Web. But they've been crippled just as much by corporate profiteering, arrogance, elitism, and encroaching dullness that have driven away readers, sometimes in droves.
>
> Newspapers must look back to have a future. They need to reclaim their populist roots—roots that the Web increasingly controls.

It's relatively easy, but not terribly useful, to write a focus statement after a piece is published. It usually comes pretty close to what's known in journalism as the *nut graf, so what graf*, or *universal graf* that summarizes the piece's main point—its focus. (Whether you're writing a long profile or a short blog item, nearly every effective piece of writing has one central point.) The challenge is to set a course for the bulk of your research or reporting early in the game.

Finding the focus means hitting the story's bull's eye. That takes as much practice in writing as in darts.

TIPS FOR A TIGHTER FOCUS

So, remember:

1. Think small: Narrow your topic to something you can report and write well in a reasonable space and time.
2. Think action: Verbs, not nouns, drive sentences and stories. Establishing your story's dominant verb or verbs can take you a long way toward establishing its dominant point. My essay, in other words, was about a verb (*to save*), not a noun (*newspapers*).

Let's try another example constructed from the Dirk Johnson story mentioned in the last chapter. Johnson showed the struggles many face quitting smoking. He did so by telling the story of one strong woman who couldn't quit, not by quoting medical studies. His story had a *point of view*, that of Jan Binder, widow, mother, athlete, and agonized nicotine addict. This point of view *humanizes* his story, engaging the reader. A focus statement of this piece should reflect her agony—which creates the story's *tension* and serves as its *hook*.

Weak Focus

It is hard to quit smoking as many smokers know. This story will tell of one smoker's struggle to do so.

Remember Stepp's advice at the start of this chapter? This focus is concise. It's expressed in two sentences. But it's certainly not arousing. It lacks the specificity needed to engage readers in Binder's struggle. It doesn't drill down to the details that engage and that help the writer or reader see the story's course. These sentences speak in generality, not specificity.

Better Focus

Jan Binder's husband died of lung cancer at thirty-seven, but she still smokes. Each day this high school athlete turned business executive struggles to beat her addiction. Her two daughters have begged her to quit, screamed at her, even broken her cigarettes in half. But like tens of thousands of other smokers, Jan Binder can't quit. This is her story.

This focus is a bit longer, yes. But here the writer and reader know that this will tell the story of Jan Binder, a story set in the universal context of all hopelessly addicted smokers. Selective facts—Binder is a young widow, a former athlete, a strong woman too weak to stop—create tension and establish the story's emotional center. Verbs convey its action. Her husband *died* of cancer yet she *smokes*. Her daughters have *begged* and *screamed*, even *broken* her cigarettes. It also establishes the piece's dominant verb: *struggle*.

Again, the focus helps the writer and editor at a news organization agree on a story's direction and establishes its hook. In doing so, it defines what information gathering remains and how the writer's lead section will resolve. It gives the story a sense of purpose, one that the essayist, amateur, or freelance writer can benefit from as much as the writer who works for a news organization.

Some writers chafe at the suggestion that focus statements should be framed before writers do the bulk of their research. By setting a course before they gather information, they argue, writers sacrifice their quest for truth with a small *t*.

I find the opposite to be true. Focus statements allow writers to look more deeply into a narrower story rather than skimming the surface in a scattershot way. They also keep that writer from careening back and forth any time an interesting (but unrelated) tangent beckons.

My pétanque story makes the point. I can't find my initial query or focus, but they clearly established the piece as being about the game's *cultural* role in everyday life.

Partway through my reporting, I interviewed a fascinating Yale University law professor by the name of Alec Stone Sweet, who gave me a significantly different perspective. During the academic year, he was a scholar and teacher in New Haven, Connecticut. In the summer, he was a highly competitive pétanque player in the South of France. At that level, he told me, the game was the domain of professional hustlers, much like pool sharks, not a meeting place in the town square for friends and neighbors to score points in the art of argumentation.

My mind raced when I hung up from our interview. Should I profile Sweet, I wondered? Or should I dig deeper into the seamier side of the game and gambling? Here my initial story pitch, reconnaissance, and focus kept me on track. Sweet's story was interesting, no question. It didn't, however, fit the interest of the publication for which I was writing (it is, mind you, the *Christian Science Monitor*), nor of my editor. By knowing my focus, I was able to identify and discuss Sweet's attractive detour without taking it. My editor and I agreed to leave it out. Had I not known my focus, I might have balled up the piece by writing about two competing threads simultaneously. It's a problem I see commonly in my students' work.

STICK WITH ONE DOMINANT THEME

Let me end with this analogy (it's almost dinnertime, so food is on my mind). Well prepared, either grilled salmon or leg of lamb can make for a delicious main dish. But the chef who serves both on the same plate will likely win few culinary awards. Both are foods. Still, they have little else in common. Two slices of a story on the same broad topic can clash in the same way. It is better to report and present one well than to cram both uninvitingly into the same space. It can ruin a reader's appetite.

Everyone needs an editor. A focus statement gives you the best shot at being your own. So go back to the memo you wrote at the end of chapter 7. Ask yourself these questions:

1. Does the story you set out to explore have a single dominant theme?
2. Will something happen to keep the story moving forward?
3. Is there a single person, place, or event that exemplifies what you are trying to say?
4. Is there an analogy that makes your main point more vivid?
5. What verb or verbs can best drive your story?

Once you've decided, write a focus statement of fifty words or less that summarizes the story line. Share it with a friend you trust to tell you honestly whether it makes sense.

NINE
INTERVIEWING FOR STORY

Questions beget stories. Curiosity begets questions. . . . Interviewing is
the most fundamental tool we have.

> —Pulitzer Prize winner Jacqui Banaszynski at the 2008
> Nieman Narrative Journalism Conference

It's hard to report a story when you aren't sure what questions to ask or
how to broach them.

My students confess they sometimes feel that way. At the seasoned age
of fifty-eight, I had a sense of how they feel as I set out on my first interview with a pétanque expert. It's not that I didn't know what to ask. It's
that I didn't know how.

I had set up an interview with Franck Filiaggi, director of La Musée Pétanque, and a representative of the largest manufacturer of French boules,
the metal balls used in the game. The problem was he spoke only French,
a language with which I have but a passing acquaintance.

And so, as I headed toward the village of Vallauris, a few miles north
of the Mediterranean along the Côte d'Azur in southern France, I carried
a tape recorder, I wrote out my questions in advance—and I prayed I
would understand at least a few of his answers.

This, I imagine, is how many interviewers must feel as they head into
the field for the first time. There's just so much to concentrate on: what
questions to ask and in what order; how to engage the subject while
frantically scribbling notes; when to interrupt for details and when to
just listen; how to stay on course but not lose the chance to probe deeper
for details; how to stay at ease yet not lose control; and, finally, how to
convey a sense of the person and place. Even for veterans, carrying out a
good interview can be a lot tougher than, say, driving a car and talking
on a cell phone, which research shows results in four times as many accidents as just driving. (Drivers on their cell phones, after all, take on just
two tasks at once.) The interviewer must concentrate intensely without
outwardly showing any of the strain of that effort.

"A friend of mine refers to interviewing as a full-body experience, where you are paying attention not only to questions and answers but . . . to what you are seeing, to what you are smelling," Banaszynski, now a Knight professor at the University of Missouri, told participants at the 2008 Nieman Narrative Journalism Conference.

Gathering information for any story requires an approach and a strategy. Mine in the case of Filiaggi was to apologize up front for my bad French, ask if I could use the tape recorder, bring along Kathy (as always), and establish my credibility by doing my homework in advance. Perhaps I couldn't speak his language, but at least I knew the rules of this quirky sport, its history, and the scene around it as it played out in the town squares of France.

To an extent, my plan worked.

Filiaggi, who has manufactured *boules* for thirty years and whose father manufactured *boules* for thirty years before him, confided in French that "my passion is not in playing pétanque. My passion is fishing." This sentence, at least, was short enough for me to comprehend and translate in my head. And the words were humorous enough for me to star mark as a possible *quote*—a sequence of words drawn verbatim from what a subject says.

When Kathy and I left, the director even gave me a book—in French, of course—by the last living descendent of the man who invented pétanque, in either the year 1907 or 1910, a matter of considerable dispute among the game's passionate devotees. I also understood his assurance that pétanque's popularity could be traced to the fact that "*tout le monde peux jouer*"—anyone can play. And they can play just about anywhere at that. Finally, I managed to comprehend a few facts, from the number of licensed players in France (450,000) to the fact that his company, OBUT, turns out 80 percent of the boules distributed worldwide.

It all felt a bit like taking notes under water. Still, I gained something from the encounter, a promising sign, I hope, for the inexperienced interviewer. Take solace in the fact that sizable obstacles won't completely cripple the would-be information gatherer entering an interview with at least a reasonable sense of the subject and a goal to pursue.

This much I can promise. Interviewing gets easier when interviewer and subject speak the same language. Taking steps to prepare for the interview help, too, in any language. Here's a start on how to map an effective interview.

1. *Focus.* Work out in advance what you want to know. Ask yourself, "What's the story and how can this interview help develop it?" Remember my day in New Jersey at the home for wayward teenage girls (see chapter 7, "Reconnaissance")? Lots of "stuff" does not a story make.

2. *Background.* Time permitting, research your topic and interview subject so you don't ask questions for which answers are readily available. ("Doing an interview is 150 percent prepping," says Banaszynski.)

3. *Prepare your questions.* Jot down a list of questions you'd like answered, taking into account how much time your subject has allowed you and what you most need to know. Then tuck the questions away, out of sight. (*Never* read off of this list; it is a surefire interview killer.)

4. *Visualize the interview.* Think in advance about the cadence and pace of the interview. Face-to-face, it's often best to ease into an interview rather than to start too narrowly or with your toughest question. Sometimes, however, two or three questions are all the interviewer will get. Then, there's no time to dawdle.

5. *Go to the subject's turf.* When possible, interview your subject in a place that tells you who he or she is. It may be in the artist's studio, the inventor's tool shed, the volunteer's soup kitchen, or the executive's office. Capture not only the person's words but also his or her surroundings. What's on the walls and on the desk? Are the furnishings sparse or sprawling, tidy or spread out? Does the artist work on one canvas at a time or several? (The answer to this question, easily observed, might lead to an interesting give-and-take on the creative process.) Is the executive's desk shipshape or chaotic, covered with a clutter of file folders and paper or neatly organized lists? Regardless of the setting, ask yourself what it says about your subject. Then ask, does it seem to verify or contradict the image he or she is trying to project?

6. *Be direct, concise, and clear.* Ask one question at a time. Forget those press conferences you've watched on TV where the reporter spends more time asking a question than the president does answering. Keep it simple. More than one question can confuse—or allow your subject to answer only the easier of the two.

7. *Listen.* Remember that your subject is the only important person in the room. The interview is about that individual, not you. You're not at an interview to converse. You are there to gather information, to hear someone else's story. This does not mean you have to be rigid or overly formal. But you should be asking the questions, not answering them.

8. *Make the subject think.* Ask questions that are "open ended," meaning they can't be answered with yes or no. Ask not, "Is pétanque a popular game in the South of France?" (If you've done any background, you should already know that, anyway.) Ask, "Why is pétanque such a popular game in the South of France?" Or, can you give an example of its popularity? Stories demand more than facts.

If your subject offers terse monosyllabic answers, say something like, "That's really interesting. Can you elaborate?" or, "Really. Can you give me an example of that?" A little interest can go a long way. Only the reporter who probes for examples can write stories seasoned with the best of them.

9. *Adapt to your subject's answers.* Prepared as you should be, surprises are inevitable. Sometimes interview subjects will show a side of themselves or a subject you never anticipated. Be prepared to adjust your line of questioning, even to detour from where you thought you were headed. ("Interviewing is like dancing," Banaszynski told me. "The other person gets to pick the music. You are leading so you've got to keep that person on the floor and flowing, but the person gets to pick the music, which means you had better listen very carefully to their music.")

10. *Don't pull punches.* Ask anything and everything you need or want to know. Journalism has two sayings that make this point: (a) "there are no stupid questions," and (b) "if your mother says she loves you, check it out." Never leave without asking the question you find most difficult or awkward.

11. *Give your subject the final word.* End by asking your subject if there's anything he or she would like to add.

12. *Stay alert when it's time to leave.* Listen intently when the formal interview ends. It's often then that an interview subject relaxes enough to reveal something hidden behind a formal guard or natural reserve.

13. *Ask permission to call back.* Once they've reviewed their notes, most writers want to follow up at least one question. Get a phone number, preferably a private one after hours, that you can call to follow up. Don't be too embarrassed to use this.

14. *Share your contact information, too.* Make sure your subject can reach you—at work or on your cell.

Note that the advice here centers around *asking* questions. E-mail can be a great tool for introducing yourself to possible interview subjects and, possibly, for setting up an interview. But *never* settle for asking a series of questions by e-mail. That is not an interview. There's no interaction, no observation, and no follow up. The writer who relies on e-mail interviews might as well pubish press releases instead.

GOING DEEPER

The most powerful stories are often the most intimate.

To get them, interviewers must sometimes coax their subjects to pull back painful scabs, reveal weakness, or confront great personal sorrow, knowing all the while that these stories will be printed for the world to see.

"For most of my adult life, I have been an emotional hit-and-run driver—that is, a reporter," columnist and author Anna Quindlen once wrote in a candid, and conflicted, piece in the *New York Times*. "I made people like me, trust me, open their hearts and their minds to me, and cry and bleed on to the pages of my neat little notebooks, and then I went back to a safe place and made a story out of it."[1]

Banaszynski, who won her Pulitzer Prize for "AIDS in the Heartland," a St. Paul *Pioneer Press* series that told the story of two male farmers and partners dying of AIDS in the 1980s, sounds a similar refrain. "I used to refer to my AIDS piece as a mutual exploitation pact," she says. "I don't think we're being honest with ourselves if we deny there's some element of that in what we do."

Reporters like Quindlen and Banaszynski don't probe their subject's pain, pull back their veil of self-protection, push for unvarnished honesty, and then write their stories out of cruelty or insensitivity. To the contrary, I have found that it is only the most sensitive and caring reporters who can tell of others' challenges or suffering without resorting to the kind of cliché that trivializes or euphemism that diminishes. Banaszynski is an example.

"I always felt if the stories I wrote had a bigger social purpose and genuinely showed my subject that they were part of that bigger social purpose, I wasn't doing a bad thing, I was doing a good thing," says Banaszynski, a big-boned, powerful woman with penetrating eyes.

Today, Banaszynski imparts that confidence of purpose to students at the University of Missouri School of Journalism. "Don't take 'no' for an answer," she tells them frequently. It's advice she has had to heed herself, often in intimate and painful circumstances. Both were the case on the afternoon of July 19, 1986, when Banaszynski and a photographer from the St. Paul *Pioneer Press* drove up to the front door of a comfortable, split-level Mounds View, Minnesota, home where less than two weeks earlier Donald Spano's wife, Beverly, and younger daughter, Jennifer, had been fatally burned in a nighttime natural gas explosion from a leaking pipeline.

Banaszynski had come to find out just what had happened and why, to answer the questions of a public concerned and curious about a story that had gripped them for days. Her deadline was that night. Her task was as difficult, as demanding, and as sensitive as reporting gets.

She had begun reporting the story the morning after the explosion, when she was assigned to profile a family cleaved in half by catastrophe. She called the public relations person in the hospital where mother and daughter, severely burned, had been taken to die.

"No one is getting access to this man," Banaszynski was told.

So, while a pack of reporters sat at the hospital, Banaszynski worked the phones, calling ministers, schools, and next-door neighbors, anyone who would get her close to the family. At 5:00 p.m., hours from deadline, she had nearly nothing.

She reached Donald Spano's aunt, then a friend of Beverly's, explaining each time, "We have to do a story and want it to be as right and as respectful and dignified as possible."

That first day's story began with the horrific happpenstance of split-second choices:

> It wasn't clear, in the confusion and grief following Tuesday's inferno in Mounds View, why Beverly Spano and her younger daughter ran out the front door to their deaths, while her husband and their older daughter ran out the back door to safety.
>
> Later that morning, at the hospital, Donald Spano told a relative as much as he could:
>
> He and his wife were awakened by an explosion that rocked their sleeping neighborhood. The smell of gas filled the house. The pre-dawn sky was hazy with smoke. They agreed to evacuate the house and seek refuge at the pond that edges their back yard.
>
> Donald Spano gathered 8-year-old Alison from her room and made his way down the stairs to the back of the split-level house. His wife went to another bedroom to get 7-year-old Jennifer, and headed out the nearest exit: the front door.
>
> —*St. Paul Pioneer Press*

Banaszynski knew that day she wouldn't rest until she had heard the story from Donald Spano himself. But he had no desire to talk. That didn't stop her. On a hunch, she called a lobbyist with whom she'd crossed paths by the name of Wyman Spano. He turned out to be Donald's cousin and, as Banaszynski persisted, "became an intermediary."

One day Banaszynski's phone rang and Donald Spano was at the other end of the line.

"I understand you want to talk to me," he told her.

ONE CHANCE TO GET IT RIGHT

"I said, 'Yes,'" Banaszynski recalls. "He said, 'Why?' . . . . That's the moment where if you can't answer the question . . . you don't get the story."

She told him he had every right to ask.

"'To be honest,' I said, 'The reason I want to talk to you is that you experienced the worst kind of tragedy in a very public way. . . . There is so much curiosity around the story that people will want to know until you tell the story.' So I didn't lie. I didn't shine him on."

Still skeptical, Spano told Banaszynski he'd give her five minutes to convince him in person at his house. She grabbed a photographer, bought a bouquet of flowers and a bottle of wine ("you don't go to a house of mourning empty-handed"), and drove there.

Sitting across from Spano in the family's living room, Banaszynski used her five minutes well.

> What I basically explained is what we do during the course of an interview. "Here is how it works. I ask a lot of questions. Some come out of left field. Some will be very painful. You have the right to say no to any question and not answer, but if you say no, I will stop and try to figure out why . . ." I let him know he had some control. It seems almost silly to say, "Here's how it works," but we never stop to explain ourselves.

She also told Spano that his story would be told respectfully and, if he chose, just once. "I told him, 'It will go over the AP wire and you will never have to do it again.' I gave him something of benefit to him."

EXPLAIN THE REPORTING PROCESS

In sensitive interviews, it is important to demystify the process, Banaszynski says. ("I've gone so far in interviews as to show someone my notebook [and say], 'Here is how I take notes.'")

She began by asking about Alison, the daughter who had survived. Then she asked Spano whether any physical injuries remained from the night his world exploded. He held up his arm to show a mild burn mark and said, "This is it," Banaszynski recalled. She asked him where the burn came from. "It's a simple question, an obvious question," Banaszynski said. "Where did you get that? Once you are in the moment and in that context, I don't think those questions are difficult." The answer would become her story's lead.

> A small burn mars the tan on Donald Spanos's forearm. It is where he cradled his daughter's head when he carried her from the fiery front yard to the cool grass behind the house.
>
> "It's from her hair, not much more than a contact burn really," he says.
>
> Physically, the burn is all that lingers of the day, almost two weeks ago, when a gas pipeline explosion ripped through Spano's life—killing his wife, Beverly, and their youngest child, Jennifer, and forever changing things for him and his surviving daughter, Alison.
>
> The light burn, probably not bad enough to scar, gives no hint of deeper wounds inflicted that day—a day Spano simply refers to as "the 8th."

"I'll never be the same person I was two weeks ago Monday," he says. "That's not fatalistic, just realistic."

—*St. Paul Pioneer Press*

Gradually, Banaszynski led Spano to the chronology of what happened the night his wife and daughter died: "I asked him what happened," Banaszynski recalls. "Once you set the table on an interview and say, 'I'm going to ask questions. Some may be hard. Some may be very painful.' Once you've done that I think the questions scare the interviewer, not the interviewee."

GETTING BEYOND THE FORMAL FIRST INTERVIEW

Still, she says, interviewing is neither a natural nor a comfortable process. When subject and interviewer first meet, they are dancers not quite in sync with the music. The awkward formality of reporter-source relationships stands in the way: the reporter there to gather information, and the subject expected to provide it. Distrust lingers. And so Banaszynski looks to move to what she calls a "second interview." Sometimes it is just that, a second interview at a second time and perhaps a different place. Or it may be a moment when a reporter leaves aside her notebook and the person being interviewed relaxes and opens up.

On this day, that second interview began when she asked Spano if she could look around the house. "At some point, I said, 'I'm having trouble envisioning this. Can you show me?'" What she saw became the paragraphs in her story that followed the lead paragraphs above.

> Everything else seems normal—even peaceful—at the comfortable home on Woodcrest Drive in Mounds View. Jennifer's ducks, Timmy and LaVerne, paddle sedately in the pond that edges the back yard. A woman's shampoo bottles and lotions clutter the vanity in the bathroom that Spano shared with his wife but that was clearly, he says, "Bev's domain."
>
> The books and games and dolls of a 7-year-old brighten the white shelves in Jennifer's room, and more dolls are stuffed into the plastic crates in her closet, resting until small hands reach out and bring them back to life. . . .
>
> It seems no different than other afternoons, with Beverly Spano and Jennifer out on one of their legendary shopping sprees. The house and those in it seem to be waiting for them to come home.
>
> But there is that burn in the crook of Donald Spano's arm where Jennifer rested her head for the last time. And a patch of burned grass discolors the neighbor's lawn as if kissed by a bit too much sun.
>
> It is where Spano found his wife and daughter after the flash.

"I think the moment the story started feeling real to me was when I walked into her bathroom and started seeing these shampoo bottles,"

Banaszynski says. "She was still there. This was so recent. Then I saw all those dolls in that crate. The notion of someone being there and gone in an instant was represented to me by those shampoo bottles and those dolls. . . . These people didn't need to be dead."

The word "flash" ends what is the first of eight "chapters" in Banaszynski's story. (See chapter 13, "Organizing Stories.") The story continued, largely chronologically, in an understated yet unblinking way that in time gives glimpses of the interaction between reporter and the man she had come to interview. This is how her fourth chapter begins.

> Spano tells his story sparingly, but directly. He doesn't flinch at the questions, but when they get too painful his answers come slowly and sometimes are no more than a word or two.
>
> Was he able to get to them?
>
> "Yes."
>
> Was he the first one there?
>
> "Yes."
>
> Was there anything he could do?
>
> A pause this time, then finally, "No."
>
> The screams had stopped by the time Spano reached his wife and daughter. Now there were only moans.
>
> "I'm no medical doctor. You always go on faith that there's something that can be done," he says.
>
> "But I knew they were burned. The clothes they had worn were no longer there. The skin on Jenny, once soft, was now hard like leather. The eyes were burned closed. The hair . . . the hair was gone."

It is in moments like this that a reporter must decide. Should I intrude with more questions or step back and allow the subject to grapple with his or her own thoughts? Will my words break the subject's train of thought? Will they intrude or insult? Or will they prompt more of the story?

WEIGHING THE SILENCE

"If you're paying attention to people and where they are you're also paying attention to where you shut up," Banaszynski says. "Sometimes the best thing is to let the silence hang."

On this day, Banaszynski recalls, she often found it necessary instead to keep probing.

"This is *visual* interviewing," Banaszynski says. "You don't get a do-over. . . . I knew he was seeing it in his head and I did ask questions very overtly because he was shutting down. . . . Your voice gets quieter, the questions get very simple and plain and they are all part of the chronology . . . what did you do next? What do you remember? What was going on?"

It was just such prompting that led the reporter to a moment in the hospital so powerful that Banaszynski struggled mightily on deadline to make it her story's lead until a friend cautioned her to back off and first provide the story's context. In the scene, Spano sat beside Jennifer in the emergency room,

> soothing her as the doctors searched her thin arms for a place to insert an in-travenous needle, telling her not to be frightened, hushing her childlike fears.
>
> "The girls had just gotten their ears pierced [Spano told Banaszynski], and we had threatened that if they didn't take care of them, they'd have to come out and the holes would close up. At the hospital they wanted to take her earrings out, and she was crying, 'No., no, my holes will close up.'"

It had taken Banaszynski ten days to get Donald Spano to return her calls. The story was one only he could tell. And he did, unflinchingly, guided by Banaszynski's gentle prodding. But he also remembered her advice, what she had told him when she first arrived: that he could say "no" and that he could keep some control himself.

At some point, Banaszynski recalled, "I told him, 'I have a very, very difficult question. You've got one hour left with your wife. . . . What do you talk about?'. . . He looked at me and started laughing and said, 'Some things are just private.' . . . It was very, very sweet."

Few interviews are this intimate, this challenging, for interviewer and interviewee alike. But nearly every depth interview has its potentially awkward moments. In their book *Doing Ethics in Journalism*, Jay Black, Bob Steele, and Ralph Barney urge journalists to both "maximize truth" and "minimize harm."[2] One way to do so, they counsel, is to ask yourself, as the writer, how you would like to be approached and treated in a similar situation.

An exercise might help you imagine just that. Think about a personal experience about which someone might want to interview you.

1. How would you want the interviewer to approach you?
2. What might that interviewer say or do to put you at ease?
3. Would anything convince you to talk, to share the experience?
4. If so, what?
5. What would turn you off?

Keeping your answers in mind, approach a friend or relative. Tell your subject that you would like to interview him about a moment or event that changed his life or perspective. Once you've established a subject, set up the interview in advance. If possible, do background work so you understand the context better.

Think about what you want to know, where you might best conduct the interview, and how you will approach the questions. Carry out the interview, going through your notes afterward to identify gaps. Then follow up, seeking details or visiting someplace with your subject that will allow you to tell the story in the most compelling way possible.

TEN
BRING BACK THE BREED OF THE DOG

It's almost always the case that the problem with narrative is that it isn't sufficiently reported.

—Adam Moss, editor-in-chief, *New York Magazine*[1]

Narrative. It's a word thrown around liberally by high-end nonfiction writers, those who borrow from the dramatic techniques of fiction and apply them to real-life stories. Perhaps that's why the mystique of narrative can intimidate newcomers to this club. Don't let it.

We've all listened to stories since early childhood. With practice, we can all tell them. The trick is to think small; to find a tightly focused tale; and, when you're ready to report, to record specifics—lots of them, more than you think you'll ever need.

Storytelling takes practice. Tom Farragher knows. Today, he is a long-form storyteller and editor of the *Boston Globe*'s Spotlight Team, its prestigious investigative unit. Like many storytellers, however, he cut his teeth on a small-town newspaper, the *Gardner News*, and built year after year from there. He learned by reading works of writers whose work he admired, looking not only at how they used words and structured scenes but also at their raw materials—the details they included in stories. He looked for small splotches of color to put into daily news stories, then dug a bit deeper to embed small scenes—known as *anecdotes*—into profiles and "Sunday stories (on Sundays, readers have a little more time and papers a little more space)."

Along the way, he made mistakes and errors of omission—he learned from them, too. In 1988, for example, as a new local reporter at the *San Jose Mercury News*, Farragher was working a Sunday shift when the editor got word that a tiny fruit fly, the Medfly, had been spotted in a neighboring town. That was big news in California, a state in which Medflies had devastated more than one hundred million dollars of crops earlier in the decade.

Farragher was assigned the story.

"I wrote," he says, "that they had discovered a Medfly in a Cupertino backyard on a fruit tree."

That didn't satisfy his editor. "She asked, 'What kind of tree was it?'" he recalls.

"It was a lemon tree," he adds. "Fruit tree or lemon tree. . . . There's a big difference." "Lemon tree" evokes an image, visual and olfactory, in the reader's brain. "Fruit tree" does not. It merely categorizes. Lemon tree shows. It was a difference Farragher remembered and sorted away, one more lesson for the next time he looked for details. Today, thirty-four years and thousands of stories since he started as a reporter, Farragher sometimes spends months reporting a single, multipart narrative series.

He still takes nothing for granted. He has learned to immerse himself in story, to fill notebooks with data, dialogue, and details that are the foundation of scene. He knows that his words must be as honest and accurate as they are dramatic and engaging; that, in writing nonfiction, both the narrative and the truth count; that no story can be better than the painstaking observation and reconstruction on which it is built.

His first instinct is always to put too much into his notebooks, knowing full well that most of it will eventually end up among the outtakes on the newsroom floor. "I want to get it all," says Farragher, whose soft-spoken, unassuming manner belies a fierce determination to get the whole story and to get it right. "No detail is too small. As a reporter, a writer, there's nothing more overwhelming than to stare at a screen and say, 'I don't have it.' So I over-report. I run out every lead I can." It is this perseverance as much as pure talent that allows him to count a Pulitzer Prize among his achievements.

Perseverance is a word that embodies the efforts of all top nonfiction storytellers: they persevere, finding their way around obstacles, road blocks, and dead ends and going back time and time again if need be to get the material to tell their stories right.

It is the last of what I'll call the "three p's" needed to tell compelling stories. We have already discussed the first two: the *planning* needed to conceive an idea, narrow its scope, and sharpen its story line; and the *preparation* that ensures the writer's information-gathering efforts will be targeted and informed by what has come before.

Perseverance means the determination to dig deep, to stay with a story until the writer can unearth what writing coach Don Fry has called the "gold coins" of reporting, the nuggets of information, anecdote, and scene that reward a reader who stays the course until a story's end.[2]

Without such details, it is much more difficult, if not impossible, to deliver what Farragher calls the "Technicolor" of stories, the sweep of setting that in their imagination puts readers into scenes. Without such details, it is hard to write with the seemingly effortless authority and confidence needed to capture readers' imagination, to steer those readers past the mere compilation of facts to the twists and turns of the story itself.

If practice and hard work are essential, would-be storytellers can take other conscious steps to sharpen the skills of finding and selecting details and images that are powerful, evocative, and, above all, true. Here are some ways to start.

Show Up

Stories can't be built on a foundation of fancy words any more than high-performance sports cars can surge from zero to sixty because of great grill work and a shiny paint job. They need an engine; the content and context of any story provide just that.

Decades ago, Gay Talese, considered the father of what was once known as "New Journalism," set out to write a profile of singer Frank Sinatra for *Esquire* magazine. Sinatra declined to be interviewed, but Talese persisted, following Sinatra wherever he could to observe the singer—to capture scene. Talese also interviewed just about anyone who would talk, from casual acquaintances of Sinatra to intimates and family members.

Once he had gathered a wealth of facts and details, Talese, the stylist, could take over. But what lets his story to this day stand among the great pieces of American magazine journalism is that each scene, each sentence, seems backed by hours of research and reporting. Talese showed up to watch the singer and to buttonhole those who knew him.

Here's how the 1966 classic, "Frank Sinatra Has a Cold," began:

> Frank Sinatra, holding a glass of bourbon in one hand and a cigarette in the other, stood in a dark corner of the bar between two attractive but fading blondes who sat waiting for him to say something. But he said nothing; he had been silent during much of the evening, except now in this private club in Beverly Hills he seemed even more distant, staring out through the smoke and semidarkness into a large room beyond the bar where dozens of young couples sat huddled around small tables or twisted in the center of the floor to the clamorous clang of folk-rock music blaring from the stereo. The two blondes knew, as did Sinatra's four male friends who stood nearby, that it was a bad idea to force conversation upon him when he was in this mood of sullen silence, a mood that had hardly been uncommon during this first week of November, a month before his fiftieth birthday.
>
> Sinatra had been working in a film that he now disliked, could not wait to finish; he was tired of all the publicity attached to his dating the twenty-year-old Mia Farrow, who was not in sight tonight; he was angry that a CBS television documentary of his life, to be shown in two weeks, was report-

edly prying into his privacy, even speculating on his possible friendship with Mafia leaders; he was worried about his starring role in an hour-long NBC show entitled *Sinatra—A Man and His Music*, which would require that he sing eighteen songs with a voice that at this particular moment, just a few nights before the taping was to begin, was weak and sore and uncertain. Sinatra was ill. He was the victim of an ailment so common that most people would consider it trivial. But when it gets to Sinatra it can plunge him into a state of anguish, deep depression, panic, even rage. Frank Sinatra had a cold.

—Esquire

Talese's riff about that cold's effect on the singer isn't speculation. Each broad statement in this lead is supported with specific scenes and examples as the story unfolds. The author's precision can be seen from the first sentence. Sinatra is holding "a bourbon," not "a drink." And Sinatra is worried that he'll soon have to sing "eighteen songs with a voice that at this particular moment . . . was weak and sore and uncertain"—not "some songs," but eighteen songs.

"In journalism, you have to show up," Talese told an admiring audience, forty-four years later at a Boston University Narrative Journalism Conference. "There are no shortcuts."[3] By showing up, he said, the writer can observe as scenes unfold before him. He can build story. The full text of "Frank Sinatra Has a Cold" is readily available at www.esquire.com, the magazine's website. I urge you to read it.

Drill Down

Not all details are equal. That Sinatra held an alcoholic drink is a detail. That it was a glass of bourbon is a lot better. (Remember the distinction between the "fruit tree" and "lemon tree" in Farragher's Medfly story?)

Small shades of detail enhance a story's authority and catch the eye of the casual reader. That's true no matter how basic the story. For example, if a gunman murders the owners of a mom-and-pop deli, execution style, after first ordering a sandwich, the writer of that story would flunk the detail test if he or she didn't ask what kind of sandwich the killer had ordered. If that writer tells the reader, "The killer paid $4.98 for a ham and Swiss on rye, ate a few bites and then opened fire," then the writer has painted a picture for the reader that, among other things, shows how cold-blooded the killer is. The extra details turn black-and-white "just the facts, ma'am" reporting into that Technicolor for which Farragher always strives.

On the other hand, it wouldn't much matter if an eyewitness reported that the shooter wore brown socks—unless a name was embroidered into one. Then, of course, the reader would demand to know what name.

If a family dog wakes up its owners, alerting them to a smoldering electrical fire in the walls of their home, the basics of the police report will not be enough. Readers will want to see how the dog reached them and where it led them. They'll want to know the dog's name, age, training, history as a pet, and breed. As this chapter's title suggests, storytellers bring back the breed of the dog.

Do Your Homework

This I'll guarantee. Before Talese set eyes on Sinatra in that smoky Beverly Hills club, he knew an enormous amount about him. Whether embarking on a daily story, a long-form profile, or a multimonth project, reporters do their homework first. They research, conduct reconnaissance that gives them deeper understanding of their subject. They establish context that informs the reporting ahead.

In 2006, shortly after the two-thousandth American soldier was killed in Iraq, Farragher set out to tell the story of posttraumatic stress disorder (PTSD) through the eyes of two soldiers who had seen the third member of their squad torn apart by enemy fire on patrol.

He met one of them, former staff sergeant Andy Wilson, while reporting a different story, a series of vignettes about a New Englander from each of the regions' states killed in Iraq.

For a while, Farragher had wanted to tell the story of PTSD through the uninterrupted narrative experience of someone suffering from the illness. Wilson, whose squad mate, Jeremy Regnier, had been killed minutes after switching positions with him in their Bradley Fighting Vehicle, seemed a good candidate.

They had dinner, and Farragher laid out bluntly how much of Wilson's life would be laid bare. "I told him, 'If we do this it will be a very intimate story and you should seriously think about it. Because if we tell your story, I'm going to want to know everything about you.'"

While Wilson weighed his proposal, Farragher headed to White River Junction, Vermont, headquarters of the national center for research about PTSD to learn everything he could about the disorder and how it affected soldiers like Wilson and specialist Dustin Jolly, the other crew member with Regnier that night. That visit would not appear in the series he eventually wrote. However, it would help inform his reporting.

Doing "homework" is not just the province of the project writer. Much simpler assignments demand preparation, too. The reporter interviewing the new high school baseball coach might ask for the coach's resume in advance and read articles, or "clips," about teams he or she coached before. These may shed light on not only the coach's experience and reputation but also his or her coaching style. It may suggest a fresh line of questioning and steer the interviewer away from questions that have been asked time and time again.

While in Provence, I prepped carefully for an interview I stumbled into with author Peter Mayle for precisely the last two reasons: to avoid obvious questions and to seek clues for those that might engage him. The topic ostensibly was pétanque. But I was more interested in how Mayle works as a writer, and I thought I might be able to pitch the interview to the *Christian Science Monitor* as a second story (see chapter 15, "Finding a Niche").

First, I reread his best-selling *Year in Provence* and then read his most recent book, *Provence, A–Z*. Next, I used my virtual access to Emerson College's library to tap into the LexisNexis academic database, where I found a half-dozen recent profiles of the British ad man turned children's book writer, Francophile, and then novelist.

This "spade work" paid off. I sold that second piece. And by the time I sat down with Mayle, I knew details about him that both helped "break the ice" and, with his confirmation, found a place in the story I wrote. I had read, for example, about Mayle's fondness for dogs, which I share; his penchant for wearing expensive loafers without socks; and his newly developed secrecy in concealing his address after resettling to a fourteen-acre estate on the outskirts of the tony town of Lourmarin. I began the story, a simple conversation with this author whose most famous book has been translated into thirty languages, by using some of this material.

> **Lourmarin, France**—He has been back in his beloved Provence for seven years now, still writing novels and nonfiction about the region's charms, its cuisine and its people. But Peter Mayle is a bit more circumspect these days about throwing his personal life open to whoever might drive by or drop in. After his first book here, *A Year in Provence*—the one that made this part of France a household word—the crush of visitors eventually drove him into self-exile for more than four years near Long Island's Hamptons.
>
> Today Mr. Mayle meets reporters in Café Gaby, a bar-restaurant in the main square of this, his second adopted Provençal village, a place in which a comfortable *mas*, or farmhouse, lists for more than $3 million with the Realtor up the street. Mayle and his wife, Jennie, live nearby, but he'd rather not say just where.
>
> —*Christian Science Monitor*

Observe as You Report

Though I had just ninety minutes with Mayle, I could in a sense extend my time by threading in what I'd read elsewhere and what I'd observed. The details a writer sees are the easiest to use. But to use them, the writer has to note them and record them. I consciously set out to see what kind of town Mayle lived in and to what extent the town acknowledged one of its more famous residents. The three-million-dollar realtor's listing helped answer the first question. The bookstore next to Café Gaby helped answer the second. The piece continued with more description of the surroundings. "Next door to Café Gaby, in the town's tabac, the works of Mayle in English and in French are prominently displayed from his famous first book about the region, published in 1989 as he neared 50, to his latest, *Provence A–Z*."

Mayle said nothing profound that morning. He hadn't published a new book that could have served as a natural focus of our discussion. Still, to the extent my piece succeeded, it worked as a snapshot, a portrait of an author back in the land he loved. Lacking a singular focus, I tried to compensate by capturing ambiance, a sense of the man and the region that captivates him.

> He arrives wearing an untucked denim work shirt and loafers, no socks, even if the shoes, as recent interviewers have noted, are Gucci (I didn't bother to ask). He apologizes for being a few minutes late, even on this morning when rain streaks down from the normally peaceful and blue Provencal sky. . . .
>
> Mayle orders a coffee and greets Gaby's dark-haired proprietor, who, he says, recently brought fresh venison to his house with a recipe for Mayle's wife to prepare it. And he chats with the ease of an old acquaintance as the conversation ranges from why the French eat so well yet stay so thin to who his favorite authors are (maritime novelist Patrick O'Brian and essayist E. B. White are two).
>
> What seems clearest is that after nearly two decades of writing about the character and the characters of Provence, Mayle's love for this rich and colorful region is undiminished. He talks of its bright blue winter skies, the wood fires and cold sunshine that set that season apart; the food, from daube to truffles; and the exaggerated nature of Provencal storytellers.
>
> But then, he is one himself.

What You Can't Observe, Reconstruct

Much reporting cannot be observed. The writer must draw it from documents, photos, and available records, and from patient, painstaking, detailed interviewing, not with just one person who witnessed an event but with as many as possible. It is the details of story that bring it to life, that put the reader in a scene. However, those details need corroboration. They need to be true.

Farragher knew some of the challenges he would face before he began his PTSD project. He knew he would have to bring back to life the fallen buddy whose memory haunted Sergeant Andy Wilson and Specialist Dustin Jolly. By then, Jeremy Regnier was long dead, blown apart as he

stood in the open hatch of the three squad mates' Bradley Fighting Vehicle on one of their nightly patrols of a sinister stretch of highway between
the Iraq airport and Baghdad's Green Zone.

For readers to grasp Wilson's and Jolly's recurring terror, the Regnier
family's loss, and the eviscerating reality of war, Farragher had to first
re-create the boy who became the young man who enlisted and then had
to take readers along on Regnier's last patrol.

"I knew from the get-go I had to make him a living, breathing, funny,
impish, imperfect person that he was," Farragher recalls.

Farragher set to work gathering whatever he could. He spent hours in
Littleton, New Hampshire, going through boxes that came home with
Regnier's remains. There were letters to his kid sister, letters that detailed
his daily life in Iraq, and a video of Regnier's memorial service in Iraq that
gave Farragher a sense of the men around Regnier, what they looked like,
and how they lived in the war zone.

At the same time, he interviewed anyone he could find who knew Regnier. "I was able to talk to teachers, and coaches and friends and relatives.
. . . I talked to people about what a smart aleck he was. That he could be a
cheap shot artist playing football around the base." As Farragher pieced
together this picture, he discovered the wrenching story of how Regnier
had ended up in the military, one of those details he knew would find its
way into print.

> As a kid in Agawam, Mass., Regnier rode bikes on dirt tracks, made forts
> in the woods behind his house and acquired a nickname after being pushed
> to the ground on a basketball court at age 11. "Toothless wonder," they
> called him after his right front tooth proved no match for the pavement. He
> shrugged it off, though, gap-toothed, he didn't smile so much any more.
>
> He was better with his hands than his head. When his father's friend, Rick
> Bertram, rebuilt a Chevy Blazer in the Regniers' garage, young Jeremy was
> a fixture at his side, ready to hand him the next wrench. Soon, the teenager
> was pulling tires and rebuilding brakes on his own.
>
> "After awhile," Bertram recalled, "I didn't even have to check on his work.
> I mean he was good."
>
> When his family left Agawam for Littleton, N.H., Regnier struggled with
> the discipline his father imposed at home and the rigor of studies that held
> little interest. He quit school, bounced around at odd jobs, drank late-night
> beers with the boys, and joined the National Guard—occasional duty that
> left him plenty of time to lounge around.
>
> In 2000, his father's patience ran out. He drove Jeremy to the Army recruit-
> ing station just down the road in Littleton.
>
> "What am I doing here?" Jeremy asked his father.
>
> "You've got two choices," Kevin Regnier remembers telling his son.
> "You're going to join full time or get the hell out." Jeremy joined.
>
> *—Boston Globe*

Ask About Anything You Don't Understand

Nonfiction writers cannot balk at asking questions that seem intrusive, insensitive, or simply dumb (see chapter 9, "Interviewing for Story"). This is no small matter for someone uncomfortable with asking questions of absolute strangers. However, the writer may need the answers. That is why the courage to ask what you do not know ranks high among the attributes needed by the would-be nonfiction writer. Plenty of outstanding reporters are shy. But they find a way to overcome that shyness. "You might be too embarrassed to ask, 'What was the color of his suspenders,'" Farragher says. "But those are the kind of details that make a story come alive."

Think Cinematically

In an early scene of the Academy Award–winning film *Slumdog Million-aire*, the older brother of the film's hero, then still a small boy, locks him in a filthy, overflowing outhouse. But the hero jumps into the pit of feces to escape in time to get the autograph of a Bollywood movie star passing through the slums. The scene is as stomach turning as it is stirring. But it establishes the boy's determined character, a theme developed through-out the film. And it does so in a strikingly visual way.

Writers, too, want their audiences to see—and to smell, hear, and feel—their characters and what they endure. By choosing imagery that appeals to the senses, the narrative writer, like the videographer, can bring those watching right to the scene.

In recounting the night Jeremy Regnier was killed, Farragher slowed the cadence of his writing, just as a videographer might slow the camera in the calm before the cataclysmic scene. He captured the heat and sounds and sense of closeness in the Bradley, the monotony and the fear of being out on patrol. He built anticipation of the horror the reader by now knew was coming.

> The Bradley . . . rolled out of the airport gate about 10 p.m.
>
> Regnier's Kenwood CD player was working perfectly and Wilson and Jolly, as they frequently did, overruled Jeremy's preference for a night of country music. So Eminem blared through their headsets, not Toby Keith.
>
> As they rumbled on Route Irish and in and out of the drab housing proj-ects adjoining the highway, Jolly and Regnier made plans to visit the gym the next day.
>
> To fight the omnipresent urge to sleep, the men drank Red Bull, gobbled over-the-counter pep pills, and puffed on cigarettes. . . .
>
> Wilson, the Bradley commander, stood in an open hatch, exposed to the early-morning air from head to mid-chest. . . .
>
> The Bradley's gun turret was not spinning, looking for targets as it would if the gunner was alert. So Wilson tapped Regnier on the shoulder.

"Hey, get up here and smoke a cigarette and let me get down there and I'll take the gun for a little while," Wilson remembers saying.

So the men switched.

It was 4:30 a.m. Their shift was nearly over.

Jolly, in the driver's compartment, chatted easily with Regnier about favorite TV shows. Jolly had just purchased the boxed set of the fifth season of "Homicide." Regnier preferred the CSI series, and Jolly asked if he could borrow his set.

In their headsets, Eminem was rapping profanely about death and dying.

Jolly steered the Bradley, making a right-hand turn into a housing project. Then he heard Regnier say, "Oh."

A split-second later, a deafening explosion rocked the war machine. . . .

The Bradley began to fill with thick acrid smoke. Jolly's eyes were burning. Wilson began to scream.

He called for Regnier. And then called again, reaching up to tug at his gunner's sleeve.

"I pull at him and he falls," Wilson remembers. "And I just (expletive) flipped. I tried my best to come across as calm. My voice was normally kind of deep. I sounded like a little girl."

Regnier, his body now slumped against Wilson, had taken a devastating hit from the jaw up.

One night in New Hampshire, nursing a beer in his motel room, Farragher read the details of an autopsy report that Regnier's father, Kevin, had given him. He could not bring himself to view the photos of the body.

Never Stop Reporting

People who write for a living can't afford to punch a clock. Their material is daily life. It doesn't start at nine or end at five.

As Farragher immersed himself in the lives of Wilson and Jolly, traveling regularly from Boston to their homes in Dayton, Ohio, and Bloomington, Indiana, respectively, he spent time with them when the tape recorder wasn't running and the pad and pen were put away. But he always paid attention.

"You never know when that detail will surface," says Farragher, who befriended Justin's grandfather and would sometimes go fishing with him.

Luck counts in information gathering. But writers like Farragher make their own luck, too, by always being alert. So it was one day when Jolly decided to send a box of Regnier's things back to Littleton, New Hampshire, where Kevin Regnier and Jeremy's stepmother lived. Farragher accompanied Jolly to the post office and catalogued the bits and pieces that Jolly had hesitated for months to give back.

Early on a frigid Saturday morning, Jolly drove his black Mustang past the fraternity houses and frozen quadrangles of Indiana University and into the lot at the Bloomington Post Office.

Inside the box he brought to the counter were some things Jolly had carefully squirreled away for Regnier's family.

A pack of Marlboro cigarettes, a canteen cover, and CDs with the music of Toby Keith, Lynyrd Skynyrd and the Red Hot Chili Peppers. Jeremy's patrol cap, his rucksack, some empty M-16 cartridges. A military headband emblazoned "Regnier." . . .

Jolly scribbled Kevin Regnier's address in Littleton, N.H., on the taped-up box.

The he looked up and asked quietly. "Do you think they'll be happy to get that?"

A few days later, Farragher was with Wilson, driving back from the funeral of a buddy in the service, when Wilson got a phone call from Jeremy's stepmother, who was in tears. She had just opened the package. The two scenes helped Farragher knit together a single story of suffering and loss from the tales of his three main characters—one dead, two in different states, haunted by that death.

Use Only What You Know to Be True

Memory can play tricks on people. And yet the narrative writer doesn't want to bog down a story with lots of contradictory information, attributed to different "sources."

In newswriting, such attribution is commonplace. One witness says the escape car was green. Another says it was blue. The reporter carefully *attributes* the information to both. "Jones said the car was green, while Smith said it was blue."

Though this is perfectly good journalism, it detracts from the storyteller's efforts to immerse a reader in his or her tale, to put the reader in the scene. Only if the information were vital (and irresolvable) would Farragher have wanted to write something like, "Wilson says the music playing was Toby Keith, but Jolly says he's quite certain Eminem was coming through his headphones."

"You want to be able to tell the reader with authority, 'Here's what happened.'" Farragher explains. "The reader knows you weren't there so you better be able to say to the reader, 'I know this.'"

Farragher established the facts of Regnier's last night not only through exhaustive interviews with Wilson and Jolly but also by talking to every soldier who had been in the jeep in front of them and by interviewing three of the four commanding officers who responded to the explosion. Most of these figures don't appear in Farragher's stories. But the consistency of their accounts gave Farragher confidence to write with authority. "If most of the people who witnessed an event agree to what happened, I will use it," he says. "If someone disagrees, I will fudge."

Farragher did one other thing to authenticate the account of the night Regnier died. On one of his trips to Fort Hood, he sought and received permission to get inside a Bradley Fighting Vehicle so he could better visualize the positions of the three men that night.

That's good reporting.

Build a Master Chronology

It can be dizzying to keep track of myriad details in a big story. That's one reason Farragher builds master chronologies when he starts a project. It's a compilation of key facts and dates that expands with time, his roadmap, and his encyclopedia. It allows him to better identify inconsistencies, discrepancies, and gaps of information.

Writers always benefit from a rough outline. (See chapter 11, "Six-Word Headlines, Ten-Point Outlines"). It charts the course of a story and lays out the main points the writer wants to include. A master chronology does more, showing gaps in information as the story is taking shape. And since most stories move forward chronologically after hooking a reader, a master chronology also gathers key dates and facts in a logical order. The facts, ordered over time, help set the story's arc and help the writer sort out key details for each story chapter.

Here's an excerpt from Farragher's master chronology for the project:

Jan. 7, 2006: Jolly mails a cardboard box containing Regnier's battlefield belongings, including a pack of cigarettes and his patrol cap, to Kevin Regnier in Littleton, N.H.

Jan. 10, 2006: Wilson eulogizes his deceased Army pal Dominic R. Coles during services in Jessup, Ga.

Jan. 11, 2006: The box containing Regnier's belongings arrives in New Hampshire. "The circle's complete as far as I'm concerned," Wilson tells the Regniers via cellphone.

Jan. 19, 2006: Jolly, who at first resisted the idea, attends his first group therapy session for PTSD.

Feb. 19, 2006: Wilson, aiming purposefully high and wide, fires his handgun at a man who had pushed him too far in a barroom on the outskirts of Dayton, Ohio.

March 31, 2006: At the Veterans Affairs Medical Center in Indianapolis, Jolly is examined by a physician who tells him, "You're just going to gradually get . . . healthier."

Get as Much as You Can the First Time Around

Reporters don't always get a second chance.

In Provence, as I sat down to write up my interview with Mayle, I knew I wanted to include the fact that he'd kept his interview appointment that day even though he would later be putting one of his three dogs, fourteen-year-old Alfie, to sleep. As I looked through my notes, however, I realized I'd missed something important: I hadn't brought back the breed of his dog. I never did get it. As I recall, I e-mailed Mayle to find out. But I didn't hear back by the time I had to file.

An important figure in Farragher's story was an army psychiatrist, Colonel Paul S. Hill, who at seventy-one had "worked hard to win a volunteer posting" in Iraq. The day of Regnier's death, Wilson sat across from the older man at his military post, the start of a relationship that Wilson told Farragher had saved his life.

Farragher reached Hill by phone one night and, he recalls, conducted a reasonably thorough interview. It was a good thing, because although Hill agreed to meet Farragher when he visited Fort Hood, the psychiatrist had second thoughts and never talked to Farragher again.

Asking people to bare their souls, particularly fragile men, damaged by war, or those who counsel them, can be a perilous business. It's one that carries great ethical responsibility for the writer.

"You look at people's lives and you have to handle (them) with care," Farragher says.

Stay Responsible to the Truth

There were times when Farragher has cried with the people about whom he was writing. In his PTSD series, there was at least one time when it looked as though the story was simply going to blow up, when Wilson, angered by something Farragher had said, announced he was pulling out.

But while the writer needs to be sensitive to the potentially exploitative nature of his work, he also has to be honest with his subjects, himself, his story, and his readers. That's why part way through the story, when Farragher noted a discrepancy between Wilson's account and Wilson's military record, the reporter had no choice but to confront his subject. Wilson had told Farragher he had placed a Purple Heart on his father's grave, one of those cinematic moments Farragher immediately knew would get into the story. But there was a problem. Nowhere in Farragher's master chronology or Wilson's military record was there any mention of Wilson's being awarded a Purple Heart, a medal given those killed or wounded in action. And so Farragher had to confront Wilson to get to the truth: Wilson admitted that he had stolen it.

The therapist who ran Wilson's PTSD group warned Farragher that telling that story could harm Wilson and damage his relationship with others in his support session. Farragher, with Wilson's blessings, held his ground. Shortly before the series ran, Wilson told the members of his PTSD group how and why he had ended up with a Purple Heart. In print, Farragher explained what had happened in a way that made the story that much more powerful. He had looked into Wilson's life and handled it with care. But he did not flinch; once again, nonfiction is about telling the truth.

This scene, in the second part of the series, takes place as Wilson wakes up in a Texas army hospital emergency room.

> Wilson only knew what he felt—possessed, immobilized, ashamed. He had left Iraq early, and he believed his superiors now considered him damaged goods. The soldier who ran when others stayed. The commander who swapped places (in the Bradley) with Regnier minutes before the bomb tore him apart.
>
> "I should have died," Wilson said.
>
> Instead, he unraveled. . . .
>
> Four days after (a fellow soldier) left Wilson's bedside, a superior officer visited him in the hospital. Wilson said he asked whether the Army considered his psychic wounds worthy of formal recognition.
>
> "I take nothing away from anybody who has lost limbs—nothing at all because they deserve more than just a Purple Heart," Wilson would later explain. "Maybe they should come up with something for us crazy guys. I don't know. But we have wounds that we're going to carry with us for the rest of our lives. I sit alone in my house sometimes and I cry like a big baby because of what happened."
>
> But the visitor to his hospital bedside, a captain, saw things differently, Wilson said. There would be no battlefield award for Staff Sergeant Andrew M. Wilson.
>
> And, he recalled, the captain told him why: "Because there is nothing wrong with you."
>
> In the days that followed, after he was discharged from the Texas hospital's psychiatric unit, Wilson returned to his limited, clerical duties at brigade headquarters at Fort Hood.
>
> In a rear storage room sat cardboard boxes full of military decorations—ribbons and badges and medals, including the one established by George Washington during the Revolutionary War to recognize those killed or wounded in action: The Purple Heart.
>
> One evening, on his way out the door, Wilson found himself unable to resist.

Details fill the notebooks of nonfiction writers. Only the most telling, the most powerful, find their way into print. We ended chapter 9 with an assignment: to interview a friend or family member about an event that in some way changed them. Now it's time to go deeper with the same material. Talk to others about the same incident.

1. Are their recollections the same?
2. Different?
3. What parts of the story can you confirm?
4. What details did you miss in the initial interview?
5. Are there any documents, letters, pictures, or other materials you can read or view to make the story more complete?

After expanding your reporting, try to build a single scene, written with a narrator's voice, that re-creates the incident. Consider it one compelling part of a larger story. The scene should be no more than a few pages long.

When you are done, read the scene out loud to a friend. Ask the friend if what you wrote makes sense. Ask if there's any place she is confused. Ask if the details you chose to include draw interest to the story, clutter the story, or distract from the story. Ask if there's something that the listener still really wants to know, something that was missing.

Then ask yourself: did you remember to bring back the breed of the dog?

Eleven
Six-Word Headlines, Ten-Point Outlines

We had spent the weekend, our third in France, in the Provençal Alps, guests of a French family that whisked us through a whirlwind of eating, activity, and merriment. We'd gorged on duck and then duck stew; we consumed a dozen loaves a day of French bread, bought fresh from the local *boulangerie* and layered with thick slabs of brie, tomme, chèvre, and other delectable cheeses whose names I never learned. Between midday and evening meals on Saturday came hours of frenetic skiing. And no sooner did we return to the chalet at sunset than did the pop of corks signal the start of the evening's round of toasts.

As Kathy and I, fresh from a few weeks of intensive conversational classes, struggled to make ourselves understood in French, our heads spun. Our instructors at the language school IS in Aix-en-Provence had conversed at something akin to a fast trot. In the ski lodge of the Bertrand family, as I'll call them, near the alpine border city of Briançon, the cross-current of conversations between the Bertrands and their other French guests raced at full gallop. Kathy and I smiled a lot, strained to understand stray words and phrases that stuck out, and bathed in the warm glow of the room.

After two exhausting days, it was time to head home. Our hostess, Marianne, who had little patience with anything as far as we could tell, suddenly veered away from the crawling traffic of the sole main roadway and, with older daughter Sophie frantically flipping through a book of maps, accelerated down single-lane roads in the pitch black, bouncing over an ancient Roman bridge and past vineyards we couldn't actually see.

In the van's middle seat, I began to wonder whether our delicious weekend would be our last. "Will we survive our personal Tour de France?" I whispered to Kathy. And in those few words, a journal entry was born.

That night, after we dragged ourselves, exhausted but still giddy, into our second-floor apartment outside Aix-en-Provence, I typed onto a blank keyboard page the headline "Surviving Our Personal Tour de France." I jotted down a few of the weekend's most vivid memories:

hugging beneath the quilt in subfreezing temperatures the first night because we couldn't figure out how to turn on the heat; standing in the snow minutes before we headed home Sunday as Marianne mopped the mountain chalet's floor clean to the front door; and careening around curves in our frenzied dash through foothills and vineyards to get Sophie back to her preparatory school before the gates there locked at 11:00 p.m.

The next day the writing came easily. It helped that the weekend remained vivid and fresh. But it also helped that the words I'd whispered to Kathy in the car had triggered a way to approach the story.

Straightforward headlines and simple outlines can go a long way toward streamlining the writing process.

The rules of headline writing are simple enough. Headlines should feed off a dynamic or "active" verb and, obviously, contain the kernel of the story's main idea.

On the other hand, story outlines to some extent depend on the nature of the piece. An outline may be a list of key images jotted down while they remain fresh in the writer's mind. Or, in a researched and slightly more formal story, it can encapsulate the key elements or chapters of the story (see chapter 13, "Organizing Stories"). A writer might start by asking these key questions in outlining the story's approach.

HOW WILL I BEGIN?

If the lead will be "delayed"—as in the Sinatra piece referenced in chapter 10 or the *New York Times'* story of the woman who couldn't quit smoking (see chapter 7)—the first outline point might sketch the key elements of the opening scene or anecdote. What images or details will make it tangible and visual? Note each in a word or two in your outline.

Here is the anecdote that began a *New York Times* article by Matt Richtel about the dangers of driving and talking on cell phones. It was part of a series of articles by Richtel that won a Pulitzer Prize for National Reporting in 2010.

> **Oklahoma City**—On his 15th birthday, Christopher Hill got his first cell phone. For his 16th, he was given a used red Ford Ranger pickup, a source of pride he washed every week.
>
> Mr. Hill, a diligent student with a reputation for helping neighbors, also took pride in his clean driving record. "Not a speeding ticket, not a fender bender, nothing," he said.
>
> Until last Sept. 3. Mr. Hill, then 20, left the parking lot of a Goodwill store where he had spotted a dresser he thought might interest a neighbor. He dialed her to pass along news of the find.

Mr. Hill was so engrossed in the call that he ran a red light and didn't notice Linda Doyle's small sport utility vehicle until the last second. He hit her going 45 miles per hour. She was pronounced dead shortly after.

Later, a policeman asked Mr. Hill what color the light had been. "I never saw it," he answered.

In this lead, Richtel develops a specific, human tale that sets up his focus by *showing* rather than *telling* the dangers of driving and cell phones. The details of the accident, Christopher Hill's clean driving record (which the reporter would have checked independently), and the two short, powerful quotes, one directly from the police report, show graphically the potential hazards of talking and driving.

An outline might have begun like this:

A. Hill's fatal accident
   1. At fifteen got cell, at sixteen got pickup
   2. Detail day of crash
   3. "I never saw it."

Why? These are key elements, things that lend power to his opening anecdote.

WHAT IS MY FOCUS?

What is my opening anecdote or scene trying to show? In other words, what will the *nut* or *so what graf*—the sentences that establish the piece's direction—say? What is the story's central thesis? Here is what followed Richtel's anecdote.

Extensive research shows the dangers of distracted driving. Studies say that drivers using phones are four times as likely to cause a crash as other drivers, and the likelihood that they will crash is equal to that of someone with a .08 percent blood alcohol level, the point at which drivers are generally considered intoxicated. Research also shows that hands-free devices do not eliminate the risks, and may worsen them by suggesting that the behavior is safe.

A 2003 Harvard study estimated that cellphone distractions caused 2,600 traffic deaths every year, and 330,000 accidents that result in moderate or severe injuries.

Yet Americans have largely ignored that research. Instead, they increasingly use phones, navigation devices and even laptops to turn their cars into mobile offices, chat rooms and entertainment centers, making roads more dangerous.

Here, the outline might have continued like this:

B. Cell phones make cars more dangerous.
  1. Harvard study (scope of accidents)
  2. Phone = equivalent of 0.08 blood alcohol level

In these three paragraphs, Richtel has established the direction, the scope, and the magnitude of his story; Hill's tragedy is one of many. Though Richtel's story appeared first in the newspaper version of the *New York Times*, the Internet allowed him to do something else: to link to the 2003 Harvard study and other research by highlighting the words "extensive research" and "Harvard" in the text. It is this capacity to embed links that makes storytelling in the digital age that much more powerful for the reader seeking depth of information. The writer can provide it for readers seeking more information without disrupting the flow of the story.

WHAT IS THE CONTEXT OF THE STORY?

Having established that the story is about the hazards of technological multitasking and driving, Richtel provides evidence showing how entrenched the problem is in American culture. Drivers, manufacturers, police, and government officials alike all bear some responsibility for the scope of the problem, he reports. That is his story's *context* and, in this type of news feature article, it typically comes immediately after the lead is established. Richtel led into this context with this paragraph:

> A disconnect between perception and reality worsens the problem. New studies show that drivers overestimate their own ability to safely multitask, even as they worry about the dangers of others doing it.

This transitional paragraph contains the seed of the next outline point, which might well be called "the disconnect." In the next seven or eight paragraphs, the author summarizes the evidence of this disconnect, beginning with these sentences:

> Device makers and auto companies acknowledge the risks of multitasking behind the wheel, but they aggressively develop and market gadgets that cause distractions.
> Police in almost half of all states make no attempt to gather data on the problem. They are not required to ask drivers who cause accidents whether they were distracted by a phone or other device. . . .
> The federal government warns against talking on a cellphone while driving, but no state legislature has banned it.

Then Richtel elaborates on what states have proposed legislation and where that legislation stands. His outline might have looked like this:

C. The disconnect
  1. Manufacturers know risks, but market things that distract.
  2. Many cops don't link cell phone use to accident causes.
  3. Though feds warn of risk, no state has banned phones in cars.
    a. What X states have done
    b. What Y states have done

In stories like this, that intersperse the personal tale with research on the policy issue it represents, writers typically go one of two ways.

- They immerse the reader in the individual's story, letting its emotional power make the author's point. Such was the case of Dirk Johnson's piece of the widow who couldn't quit smoking (See chapter 7, "Reconnaissance").
- They move thematically through the story, using personal example and anecdote to show key informational points but focusing as much on fact as story.

Richtel's story takes the second approach. His next section, for example, looks at the perspective of scientists who have studied the distracted driver and the implications of their research to policy.

Still, he doesn't forget Hill, returning to his tragedy at the end of the story's first section (and elsewhere, including the story's end).

> [Hill] pleaded guilty to negligent homicide, a misdemeanor, for the death of Ms. Doyle. Now, when he is a passenger in a car, it makes him nervous when the driver starts talking on the phone. But Mr. Hill, who is polite and deferential, said he doesn't want to badger drivers about the risks.
> "I hope they don't have to go through what I did to realize it's a problem," he added.

(If he wrote a chapter-by-chapter outline of his piece, Richtel undoubtedly gave close consideration to how and when he would work Hill back into the piece.)

TIME AS AN ORGANIZING PRINCIPLE

Other writers, after hooking the reader, allow their stories to unfold in a series of scenes or chapters that stay within chronological time. In such cases, an outline can use the technique of Tom Farragher's master chronology, listing key dates, facts, details, and scenes under subheads. (See chapter 10, "Bring Back the Breed of the Dog"). The chronological outline serves as the writer's muscle memory without stilting the writing itself.

A shorthand of key points allows the writer to draft without worrying about gaps of content.

Whatever an outline's form, its goal remains the same. It is meant to keep the writer on track, to allow the writer to see the story in subsets small enough to build on or, if necessary, to disassemble and move around as the writer plays with structure. It is far easier to shift bullet points, for example, than massive blocks of type.

As I did in writing up our adventure in the Alps, I'd urge you to start with something even more basic than the outline: a single-line headline, a half-dozen to, at most, a dozen words long.

HEADLINES AS A FORM OF FOCUS

Headlines help establish focus. In the Internet age, they can also prove vital in drawing readers; a growing number of news websites offer nothing but headlines on their home pages. Clear headlines are imperative in the blogosphere where spiderwebs of linked headlines can increase readership exponentially. For example, after the Port-au-Prince quake, I wrote a blog titled "It's More Than a Matter of Semantics," criticizing the news media for calling those Haitians who had taken food from a destroyed market "looters." About sixty people read it. When the *True/Slant* news editor led the home page with the post, retitling it "Don't Call Haitians Looters," I drew more than a thousand "hits" more, many of them likely linking to the post through everything from personal websites to the *Atlantic* magazine's website.

That experience reminded me of what a big difference a headline can make. Still skeptical? Let's take a look at the August 20, 2009, home page of that all-American, shoved-under-the-door-of-your-Holiday-Inn newspaper, *USA Today*. It gives nothing but headlines to draw "surfing" readers into the stories. The verbs, in each case, are italicized.

1. Polls *Close*, Counting *Begins* in Afghanistan
2. Mortgage Delinquencies *Rise* to New Record
3. Scotland *Lets* Ill Lockerbie Bomber *Return* Home
4. Ailing Kennedy *Asks* for Speedy Succession
5. Credit Card Holders *Get* More Notice on Rates, Fees
6. Mercury *Found* in All Fish Tested from U.S. Streams

What these headlines hold in common offers clues to how a headline works:

1. All headlines summarize the story's main point.

2. All follow basic subject-verb-object sentence construction. (Take the fifth headline: the noun is "holders," the verb is "get," and the object, a direct object in this case, is "notice.")

3. All but one of these headlines, the last, is in the *present* tense. This gives a sense of immediacy to the story. (In the final example, the headline writer could have recast in the present tense by writing, "Researchers *Find* Mercury in All Fish Tested from U.S. Streams.")

4. All the verbs are "active." Something concrete happens. The verb "to be" and its forms, such as "Voting *Is* Over in Afghanistan," would be flat in comparison (as was my original headline on the Haitian "looters" post). It gives less specific information in a less dynamic way.

5. All the headlines are concise—well, almost. In the second headline, the word "new" is redundant. All records are new because a record means something that hasn't happened before.

6. All are skeletal sentences. All headlines demand active verbs and at least implied nouns (in "Surviving Our Personal Tour de France," "surviving" takes the place of "we survive"). On the other hand, headlines omit articles such as "the," "a," and "an." It is "polls close," not "the polls close." Whether they are redundant or not, adjectives, such as "new," which modifies the noun "record," should be used sparingly, as should adverbs, which can usually be eliminated by choosing a more specific verb—delinquencies *rise*, they don't *go* (the verb) up (the adverb).

These headlines hold one other key element in common. They both "tell" and "sell" the story.

On other websites—at Salon.com or at the Washington Post (www. washingtonpost.com), for example—headlines are often accompanied by a single, short, sharp sentence that serves to summarize and tease the reader to click for more. (These typically reflect the kind of focus statement discussed in chapter 8, "Honing the Focus.") Either way, knowing and summarizing a story's main point draws readers. At the same time, however, good headlines help organize and focus the writer, especially one who has yet to put a word on the page.

A SIX-WORD SUMMARY

This bit of wisdom predates the Internet age. Crusty city editors have long challenged their reporters to summarize their stories in a sentence on the back of a business card. "If you can't write a six-word headline, you don't have a 600-word story," more than one veteran editor has said.

In establishing focus, a sharp, direct headline need not dictate a story's tone. Direct headlines can work atop fast-paced news and atop stories that take a less direct route. On the same day it posted the headlines above, for example, *USA Today* took a look at the factors driving heated opposition to the Obama administration's health care plan. That story's headline, "What's Fueling Town Hall Anger," took a direct approach even though the writer took a slower, storytelling approach.

Anecdote

For Dave Swift, the frustration started with last year's $700 million bank bailout. For Andrew Molaison, it was the sense his taxes were subsidizing people who bought homes "totally beyond their means."

In Northeastern Pennsylvania Swift found like-minded neighbors at a Tea Party "Patriots" rally. He stayed in touch with the anti-tax group.

Along Mississippi's Gulf Coast, Molaison used the Internet to connect with a local chapter of the 9/12 Project, which is sponsored by conservative talk show host Glenn Beck.

Nut Graf

Those first steps led both men, 1,200 miles apart, to congressional town hall meetings on health care this week. The two are part of a phenomenon enabling national conservative groups to galvanize grass roots anger about big government and reshape the debate over President Obama's health care plan.

Suddenly it's the conservatives' turn to be fired up.

—*USA Today*

This example reflects an important reality of contemporary news. In the surfing culture of the Internet, a concise, direct headline can focus writer and reader alike without interfering with the story's tone or approach. Because headlines and outlines, like focus statements, are compact, they can be readily changed or reorganized as new information dictates. In a way, this book serves as an example. When I first sent out a proposal to write it, the book had a different title and was eight chapters long. The chapter outline later grew to twenty and then shrank back to fifteen. Each time I reviewed my proposal, I was forced to take measure of how my approach and the book's shape had changed. The book's shifting table of contents served as an outline of sorts, helping me work out whether its chapters were logical and sequential. (I can't guarantee I've succeeded; you'll be the judge. But I tried. I did not simply sit down and start writing.)

I outlined the story of our ski adventure, too. But besides the headline, all I needed was a few key images. Sometimes, when a story's focus dawns clear in a headline, the writing comes quickly and comfortably (see chapter 12, "Drafting Fast"). It will likely still need revision. But as I've said before: know where you are going and you'll get there a lot faster. That, is something we were reminded of on our wild car ride as Marianne twisted and turned on a route she invented as she drove. Here is how the piece began:

It didn't matter that my legs ached after a day of downhill skiing. Or that we'd eaten no dinner. Or that I badly needed to pee. This car ride was worth every bit of discomfort.

After four hours, two abrupt U-turns on narrow roads, one 360 degree loop to loop, one rattle across an ancient car-wide Roman bridge, and several hairpin turns on pitch black roads too small to crack the average French road map, we arrived back in Aix. After a passionate, if often opaque, conversation about adoption, journalism, philosophy, and truth, carried out in the fog of two languages, amid the turns and twists of our tortuous trip, our marvelous weekend with the family Bertrand had reached its end.

There were moments, I confess, when I took comfort in the fact that at least we had a cell phone to call from should our car end in a ravine or, worse yet, a river. But then I should have had more faith in the indomitable Marianne Bertrand. She is a woman in perpetual motion, the mother, chauffeur, drill sergeant, and guide of three children and a soft-spoken international businessman named George, who has been her longtime companion and a second father to her kids.

But let me start at the beginning.

This is the end of my journal entry's first section. It established that this madcap car ride would frame this story and established Marianne Bertrand as its main character. Though we are going back to "the beginning," in this case a section about who this family is and why we were with them, I tipped the readers that this ride wasn't over. If I had not returned to it, I would have cheated the reader.

The next section was written to give context to this tale, by developing both the family members and their family culture, which defies stereotypes of leisurely life in the South of France.

We had come to know the Bertrands through a wonderful bit of serendipity. A year ago, a former graduate student told me her cousin knew of a French student interested in spending three weeks in the United States. We jumped at the chance to be her host, knowing that we'd be heading to France in January for five months. What we didn't know was that our visitor, Marianne's oldest child Sophie, for years had passed the apartment we'd rented in the hills above Aix every morning on the way to school or that her family would adopt us on our arrival.

The Bertrands are a family of strong women. Sophie, who turned nineteen last week, is studying chemistry, physics, and mathematics about seventy hours a week in preparation for exams that, if she passes, will gain her admission to one of France's top universities next fall.

Precise, organized, a problem solver by nature, she is the map reader and guide on mamma's impulsive cross-country adventures. Her younger sister, Anna, is outgoing, fun-loving, and, on skis, very, very fast. At sixteen, Anna skis the five thousand foot vertical drop of the ski resort near their ski chalet in seven minutes, according to Sophie.

Their younger brother, Gilbert, twelve, lets his mother and sisters run the show.

Marianne, a single mother since the children were young, is her family's glue and standard bearer. "I'm strict," she told us matter of factly on our first visit to her house after we complimented her on her gracious and well-behaved children.

Indeed, she is. And organized.

So as we clutched our seats and wondered what lay around the next turn of our personal Tour de France, we reminded ourselves that this was the woman who picked us up at the airport, stocked our refrigerator on our arrival (stores are closed on Sunday), instructed her kids to slow down when I got tired on the slope, and ordered Kathy and me, her guests, out of the ski chalet ten minutes before we headed home so she could mop the floor right to the door. And this is a woman who is a high-level officer of an Aix business, owns several rental properties (between kids and realtors, the "boing, boing" sound of her cell phone goes off with regularity), and does things right, or not at all.

Indeed, those with the mistaken notion that French *joie de vivre* can be equated with a relaxed and lazy lifestyle should spend an hour with Marianne Bertrand. Or drive for ten minutes on French roads. Or navigate a ski slope in the French alps. It is the British who politely queue in lines. The French are in a hurry.

TRANSITION BETWEEN POINTS OR THEMES

From this point the story moved chronologically through the weekend, ending back in the car. The transition was simple enough:

> Our weekend adventure started on Friday evening . . .

The transition from weekend back to car ride was also simple, again using chronology as my ally.

When we returned to the chalet from the slopes at 4:30 p.m. on the second day, Marianne had organized the army to head home.

And we were off.

Sophie again rode shotgun; Kathy and I sat in the second seat. . . .

I offered to help with the driving. Marianne politely, but firmly, said no.

"It's difficult with all the roads," she said with a wave of her hand. "We might miss a turn."

I didn't realize how true that would prove.

About ninety minutes into what should have been a three-hour trip, the traffic simply stopped—too many cars merging on roads too small to absorb them. Given that we were still in the alps, the only practical solution was to wait.

But that required patience. Marianne abruptly turned right and gunned into a nearby village with a fountain in the town square and little else. There, she rolled down her window and grilled an unsuspecting resident, parking his car. We couldn't catch half her words but she sounded like a reporter putting a squeamish politician on the hot seat. The thrust of her questions was clear enough—was there any way over the mountains to escape the long line of cars ahead of us?

The man looked increasingly bemused and Marianne finally relented.

"OK. We'll go back to the main route because Jerry will think I am crazy," she said, in French, a slightly crazed twinkle in her eyes.

But it wasn't thirty minutes before we bolted off the road again, this time through a dark valley of fruit trees and vineyards somewhere in between Gap and Sisteron. Sophie stared intently at the map as Marianne careened around corners, over the Roman bridge and in and out of various roads that sometimes ended nowhere. By the time we found ourselves just outside of Sisteron, across the Durance River from the line of headlights still strung like Christmas decorations on the main two-lane road, I'm not sure we had saved a minute. But our adventure had certainly been more entertaining than the Sunday night crawl.

"I wonder, Marianne," I asked her in French, nodding toward the river, "whether your car can swim?"

In the front seat, Sophie just rolled her eyes.

"Don't," she said, "give her any ideas."

Did my story fit the headline? What do you think?

Now it's your turn. Take ten or fifteen minutes to craft three or four single-line headlines for the story you began to craft after chapter 10.

Show them to a friend and ask these questions:

Now jot down at least ten key points in an outline that you might use to complete the story. They can be themes in the story or subheads beneath these themes. (See the outline for cell phones and cars above.)

Finally, deconstruct the single scene you wrote after chapter 10 and abbreviate it in outline form.

1. Do your headlines summarize the story?
2. Do they build off an active verb?
3. Are your headlines in the present tense?
4. Do any of your headlines lure your reader in?
5. How?
6. Which headline do you think works best?
7. Why?

TWELVE
DRAFTING FAST

Sometimes it pays to be bold, to head off like a teen in a red convertible with the top down, cruising. This isn't quite the chaos of freewriting (see chapter 2, "A Little Jazz"). You've got a rough idea of where you want to go (the beach, presumably). You've got a focus if not an entirely formal one (if you're really in a red convertible, that focus varies by gender).

And ideas are spilling out so fast that it would be a shame to go through your notes one more time to star mark good quotes, underline illuminating details, and earmark important facts. That's when it is time, as writing coach Don Fry used to say, to "draft fast to block the internal censor"— that gnawing whisper in your ear that tells you your story may just not be good enough.

Hooey.

As a writer blocked since birth, or so it sometimes seems, I tend to measure momentum by the number of essays I'm drafting fast and polishing later. When I can squeeze words from the faucet at more than a drip, they seem to get cooler and fresher, not just more frequent.

Is it illusion? Who knows? But at least those words are more fun to write. I know I'm not an anomaly of one. I've got lots of classy company.

Take Anne LaMott, author of *Bird by Bird*. "For me and most of the other writers I know, writing is not rapturous," she writes. "In fact, the only way I can get anything written at all is to write really, really shitty first drafts."[1]

Take songwriter Terence Martin. I've never met him; I don't even own his CDs. But last week I tuned into a show on WUMB folk radio 91.9 FM in Boston called "The Art of the Song." And there was Martin, a folkie, poet, and school teacher, wishing out loud that he could be more prolific. He told two stories that stayed with me. The first was about his students, sixth graders and tenth graders, he said. The sixth graders have boldness, creativity, and confidence in writing that has disappeared by the time they get to high school. The tenth graders are more cautious, less willing to put themselves out there. Metaphorically, they've stopped drafting fast.

Then he told a story about himself. He said he asked a friend, another songwriter with whom he sometimes writes, how he could be so prolific. The man responded with something like, "I don't care." Whether his work was good, bad, or indifferent didn't matter. He took joy in the process of creating.

ONE APPROACH DOESN'T FIT ALL

In truth, we all care. We write not only for its own sake but also because we want people to read us—and to like what they read. By we, here, I mean everyone who writes. I'm convinced, however, that writers part ways when it comes to how they write most effectively. In coaching journalists in newsrooms and at writing conferences, I've gotten some understanding of these differences. Most reporters, trained to focus first, labor long over their lead section. It sets their story's tone and direction. But I've met writers who can't start a story until they've figured out where they'll end, and writers who begin by blocking scenes randomly and organizing them roughly in midstory before tackling beginning or end.

In sharp contrast, I once worked with an excellent investigative reporter who worked so methodically that, by the time he wrote, he'd work his way through a detailed outline, containing not only main points but also key facts, quotes, and details. Everything was in place except perhaps the transitions and the pace and cadence of the words. This reporter never "drafted fast."

Then there are writers like me, those who bleed when they move too slowly, those prone to paralysis when they feel the weight of wanting to get things right the first time through. If you, too, are like that, whether a professional, amateur, or student, it helps to follow Fry's advice, to tread lightly through those earlier tips about headlines and outlines, to let your fingers fly.

Try it when you're inspired by an idea crystallized in the space where you think best (see chapter 1, "Finding a Place—and Space—to Think"). Try it the day after you read through all your notes on a long reported piece—and then got stuck trying to organize an outline. Try it to dislodge the mud that's started to dry around your story before you've even got the main idea down.

Drafting fast works best for me when I know where I'm going to start and, best off, where I'm going to end. I'll sometimes solve these problems walking the dog or riding my bike. Somehow, as I move through geographic space, I free the ephemeral space of my subconscious and ideas tiptoe in, catching me by surprise. I've learned to capture them quickly—on tape, a scrap of paper, or if it's handy, my computer. This is drafting fast. It's rough, spontaneous, and in need of revision. The flip-side, I find, is that the words and thoughts are fresh.

How important, how reliable are our special spaces to think? For me, they are essential. A few years ago, the day after visiting an aging cousin at a rehabilitation center, I walked to the post office to mail a letter. As I walked, an essay started percolating in my brain. I got home eight minutes before I had to leave for work and used seven of them to draft the words below. They were just a start, but a decent one on a blog post that family members e-mailed across the country.

"EVERYBODY'S AUNT PEG"

She's my second cousin by marriage or maybe my first-by-marriage-once-removed. No matter. For as long as I can remember, she's just been Aunt Peg. Everybody should have one. She turned 95 this March and now lives in a nursing home in Marblehead, Mass. But that's only temporary, during her recovery. You know, from hip replacement surgery. Her second in two years. And she is recovering. . . .

"How are you, deah," she greeted Kathy and me on the July 4 with a big smile, a hint of her native New Rochelle, N.Y., still breaking through. It was time for music, singing, laughing and memories. With Aunt Peg, it always is. She played the violin every day into her 90s. And though her short-term memory is largely shot—"do you sing, too" she kept asking my brother Dennis—she can still sing the words and tunes of the old-time favorites. Two days after surgery, she began knitting a beautiful blue wool pullover.

Life hasn't always been easy for Aunt Peg. She lost her husband 30 years ago and a son to cancer in his 50s. You'd never know it from her smile. It rarely deserts her. Her "Carlie" was a man of wit, dash and letters, a man who took his young children to Ireland to try his hand at writing. But he had his demons, too, including a penchant for the nip. That's long forgotten in Peg's memories. She loves the story of the first time they met, when he heard her perform and drove her home in a Cadillac. He wasn't much of a dancer then either but he got better; she suspects he took lessons between their dates.

Peg's reach goes deep through the generations. The last time I visited her, Andy, one of her grandsons, played the piano for her for two hours. (Music flows through the family's veins; Peg's brother was a professional trumpet player. . . .) A granddaughter, also in her mid-20s, visited her nursing home three times alone in the last week, coming all the way from Cambridge. But then, in a subtle way, Peg is the glue that has brought us all together on holidays—from Thanksgiving and Christmas to Father's Day and July 4—for a good long while now.

It was time to catch the bus, which I did that morning filled with energy. For me, these paragraphs were an awfully good seven minutes. And I was confident that at least one section—"for as long as I can remember, she's just been Aunt Peg. Everybody should have one"—would be a keeper. Why? Because somewhere in our memories, we do all have one. The line established the "universality" of the piece without announcing it.

Two years after I wrote this piece, Aunt Peg died as she was being wheeled into the hospital for a routine medical test. Her heart stopped. Her daughters, my second cousins, asked me to deliver her eulogy. I was honored, and I suspect the piece I'd begun before work that July morning had something to do with it.

I like blogging, as I suspect millions of others do, too, because it carves the virtual space for me to store journals and essays that before would be scattered about on scraps of papers or travel notebooks stuck in a drawer to yellow. Before I began posting at *True/Slant*, I would write these essays for myself, on www.blogger.com, but sometimes friends, relatives, and former students stopped by. Then and now, I like the fact that blogging leaves room for the unfinished thought. Not all blogs need to be complete, let alone polished. In some ways, they can be a repository for string (see chapter 4, "Gathering String").

Here, for example, is a blog I titled "Bits and Pieces" and posted while in Aix-en-Provence.

A few odds and ends:

- In France, le chien est le roi (the dog is king). Dogs sit in restaurants; shop in Monoprix, the Target of Aix-en-Provence; ride on buses, sidle along sidewalks and leave *les crottes* (use your imagination), wherever they damn well please. Dog watching competes with people watching. Missing, alas, are signs that warn: "Walk, at your own risk."
- At the corner *epicerie*, or grocer, we bought some wine, cheese, dried fruit, cereal and cleaning materials today, including Monsieur Propre (Mr. Clean to you). "Cinquante-quatre-trente-trois," rattled off the cashier. I stared, bewildered. "Cinquante-quatre-trente-trois," she repeated. This time, I sort of got it—50 something (actually 54.33)—and handed her three 20 euro notes in triumph. Such little victories are important, especially on a day when I mistakenly used the word for buttocks (*la fesse*) in class instead of the third-person subjunctive for "to make" (*fasse*).
- I've developed a nodding acquaintance with an old fellow at the end of our bus route home. He has a drooping handlebar moustache and a whimsy to him that's typical of what I call the watchers, the mostly older men who gather in cafes or on boule courts or stand in small clusters along the sidewalks. My new acquaintance sits on the

same stone wall each day, smoking a hand-rolled cigarette. We've progressed to exchanging smiles and *bonjour*.

• This is a city of high-end boots and higher-end pastries. Pointy-toed, pencil-heeled, primary-colored and plush, the shoes in storefronts are something to behold (as are the women who wear them). As for the pastries, real cream squirts from inside. And the chocolate is so rich its fragrance bewitches.

Drafting fast does not mean developing complacency. A fast draft is no more. By the time I posted the piece on Aunt Peg, I'd spent several more hours revising and polishing it. A good fast draft, however, gets to the heart of the story while it's still pumping. The craftsman in the writer can dissect and refine later.

In 1995, I found myself on opposite coasts from Kathy on our twenty-fourth anniversary. I started drafting a letter that was initially meant to be between us. That summer, however, Kathy was three thousand miles away in California. I was working as the intern adviser for the *Boston Globe* newsroom. And so, as I wrote, the letter gave birth to a column, one that Kathy still has in her drawer. Three drafts later, it read like this:

"LOVE TOOK ITS TIME, BUT CAME TO STAY"

She wasn't love at first sight, this brown-haired girl with freckled face and speckled eyes. But as she stood at the front desk of Grand Lake Lodge, Colo., dressed in frayed cutoff jeans and a beaten-up blue ski jacket, I was drawn to her smile.

She asked if I'd fashion a clothing rod for her rustic cabin, and I managed somehow, just the first time I would fool her that summer. The second came a few weeks later, when I cooked steak, potatoes and corn-on-the-cob over an open fire. I didn't tell her that boiled eggs were my only other entrée, or that it took me an entire eighth-grade semester to make one miserable wooden coat hanger in shop.

But then, there was no hurry to this relationship; patience is Kathy's way. I broke our first date; it was the other girl's birthday. On the second try, we walked out of a bad movie. The third time we borrowed a car and Kathy drove me 50 miles over the Continental Divide to a podiatrist who could treat my plantar warts.

Sleepless in Seattle this was not.

My foot, however, was a mess, and those 50-mile drives became a weekly routine. As Kathy negotiated the winding pass—I had no license—we'd talk of politics and philosophy, of books and beliefs, of family and growing up. I had other thing in mind high atop the star-lit passes; patience has never been my middle name. Kathy, as always, prevailed.

That was 27 years ago. I was 19, she an older woman of 20. It took three years of letters and leavings before we married at my parents' house on a

Vermont hillside. She showed up late, driving in a white lace gown with a bull mastiff beside her. Her family was later yet, a statement perhaps of what her Iowa-bred Mayflower stock thought of us New York nothings.

We returned from a glorious European honeymoon to an uptight life in a one-bedroom box of an apartment in Stamford, Conn. There were dinner parties, bridge games and a doubles tennis match in which my partner crowed in triumph when her net shot nearly castrated her husband. This was marriage? At year's end, we emptied our water bed with a garden hose from a second-floor window and headed back to Colorado.

Twenty-three years and 12 moves later, we find ourselves on different coasts today. It's our 24th anniversary, our first apart. I thought it a good day to say that in a way, at least until the next time she's late or the next time I forget to empty the garbage, we're more in love now than then. I'd like to think I've helped Kathy to laugh more, to speak her mind. She's taught me to listen and to wait, at least occasionally. And we've learned together as we've traveled, raised two kids, moved and changed jobs. Kathy's a private sort, so on this day it wouldn't do to tell her, "I love you," for all of you to see. Instead, I'll say, "Let's not do this again."

This summer, I had an opportunity to work for *The Globe*. Our daughters, Betsy and Meghan, had our promise to return to Palo Alto, Calif., from where we moved a year ago. So with Kathy they headed west from our new home in Syracuse, N.Y., while I headed east.

Work has been interesting; I can't complain. But in the evening, I miss Kathy's animated discourse on what she's reading (always something). I miss her smell, her touch. I miss, sort of, the blunt remarks about the words I write. And when I wake in the morning in a single bed, I miss the sight of a Midwestern girl with freckled face and speckled eyes, her face opening to a smile etched by the lines of time.

—*Boston Globe*

It's your turn to draft fast. Start by asking yourself these questions:

1. What new string has filled my notebook in recent days?
2. What single image from the last week has stayed with me? Why?
3. What's on my mind when I wander into the mental spaces where I think best?
4. Am I working on a story, mostly researched, on which I'm stuck?

The answer to any of these could lead to a story or essay worth drafting fast. Take a stab at writing a single-line headline first. Jot down a few elements you'd like to include. Then, write like the wind.

Thirteen
Organizing Stories

All writers want their stories to have impact. As he sat down to write about the potentially dangerous processes of preparing and distributing ground beef, Michael Moss must have known he faced a tough sell. Why would readers care? On the one hand, he had a broad potential audience: who hasn't eaten a hamburger at a family cookout? On the other, few spend time worrying about the odds of getting sick from eating one.

Moss did what writers often do: he looked for a powerful and personal way to *show* readers what his research *told* him. He needed a strong character and a compelling anecdote to convey the urgency of his broader theme: that premium ground beef readers buying in the "angus only" section could be downright hazardous. His article in the *New York Times*, which won the 2010 Pulitzer Prize for Explanatory Journalism, began like this:

> Stephanie Smith, a children's dance instructor, thought she had a stomach virus. The aches and cramping were tolerable the first day, and she finished her classes.
>
> Then her diarrhea turned bloody. Her kidneys shut down. Seizures knocked her unconscious. The convulsions grew so relentless that doctors had to put her in a coma for nine weeks. When she emerged, she could no longer walk. The affliction had ravaged her nervous system and left her paralyzed.
>
> Ms. Smith, 22, was found to have a severe form of food-borne illness caused by E. coli, which Minnesota officials traced to the hamburger that her mother had grilled for their Sunday dinner in early fall 2007.
>
> "I ask myself every day, 'Why me?' and 'Why from a hamburger?'" Ms. Smith said. In the simplest terms, she ran out of luck in a food-safety game of chance whose rules and risks are not widely known.

Stephanie Smith's story is tragic. But the story Moss published in fall 2009 ultimately was about more than one bad hamburger or one individual's bad luck. He used her story to tell a more universal tale, one that can

119

affect any of us: the safety standards for processing and distributing meat, and particularly ground beef, fall far short of what we might expect.

TWO APPROACHES

When writers use one person's story to make a bigger point, they have a choice. They can keep their focus narrow, calculating that the power of the individual story will carry an implicit message to readers of a bigger problem. Or they can use the individual story to draw more explicit connections to the bigger issue. Moss took the second course, first using Smith's graphic example to draw readers to his story, then supplying evidence so meticulously researched and compelling about the scope of the problem that I didn't eat a hamburger for a half year after reading it.

In early 2008, Brendan McCarthy, one of my former Emerson students, took the first approach. He wrote an eight-part series about the thirty-seventh homicide victim in New Orleans that year. His series, which conveyed one city's scourge through one family's loss, was a finalist for a Pulitzer Prize in 2009.

The first "chapter" of his first installment began and ended like this:

> The boy, fresh-faced with no stubble, lies in the gutter, his white shirt soaked in blood and rain. One shoulder rests on the sidewalk, the other on Frenchmen Street.
>
> A fluorescent glow from a corner store awning stops just short of the 37th homicide victim of the year, shot dead in the 7th Ward, one of New Orleans' most violent neighborhoods.
>
> Police Detective Anthony Pardo had left work hours earlier, anxiety gnawing at his gut, not knowing where the next body would drop. He just knew he'd have to be there immediately. Pardo's name sat at the top of the homicide division's Up List, meaning he would take charge of the next victim, from curbside to courthouse. When the inevitable call crackled over the radio—signal 30, a homicide—Pardo and his partner, Harold Wischan, dropped half-eaten dinners and family conversations. They donned fresh suits and headed out into the mid-March night to tend to another family's nightmare. . . .
>
> Tonight's case bears the hallmarks of so many others in a city that year after year posts among the highest per-capita murder rates in the nation: young black males, shot at night, right in the street, right in front of people.

The paragraph above is about as far as McCarthy ever strayed from his narrative of a single homicide, a single family's grief, a neighborhood's silence, and the frustration of the detectives trying to bring a murderer to justice. In his case, the pure narrative of events remained at the story's center, not merely as the frame of a broader story on elusive justice on the mean streets of contemporary New Orleans. The story's scenes and raw emotion, rather than its contextual facts, carried the reader along. McCarthy made no attempt to tap experts or draw on data to build an authoritative picture of justice and violence in the city.

In his *New York Times* story, Moss took a more traditional, if equally demanding, journalistic approach. He uses the anecdote of Smith's accident to grab readers' attention and then immediately makes the point of the anecdote explicit in two anchoring paragraphs—the *nut* or *so what grafs* that tell readers why they should care. These paragraphs anchor and broaden the story by spelling out the story's overarching theme and providing evidence to support it.

> Meat companies and grocers have been barred from selling ground beef tainted by the virulent strain of E. coli known as O157:H7 since 1994, after an outbreak at Jack in the Box restaurants left four children dead. Yet tens of thousands of people are still sickened annually by this pathogen, federal health officials estimate, with hamburger being the biggest culprit. Ground beef has been blamed for 16 outbreaks in the last three years alone, including the one that left Ms. Smith paralyzed from the waist down. This summer, contamination led to the recall of beef from nearly 3,000 grocers in 41 states.
>
> Ms. Smith's reaction to the virulent strain of E. coli was extreme, but tracing the story of her burger, through interviews and government and corporate records obtained by the *New York Times*, shows why eating ground beef is still a gamble. Neither the system meant to make the meat safe, nor the meat itself, is what consumers have been led to believe.

Both Moss's and McCarthy's approaches to telling a story can work. And either can leave readers feeling cheated. When writers, like Moss, use one person's example to make a broader point, they can't just dangle the individual tale in the lead to titillate and then forget about the individual character that lured readers in. Instead, that character needs to be threaded throughout the story, both to provide examples of broader points the writer makes and to resolve the individual's situation.

As he leads his reader through the details of how meat is processed and where federal oversight has broken down, Moss keeps his eye on both Stephanie Smith and the story of the specific meat she ate. He references where the trimming in "Ms. Smith's burger" came from ("a slaughterhouse in Uruguay, where government officials insist that they have never found E. coli O157: Yet audits of Uruguay's meat operations conducted by the U.S.D.A. have found sanitation problems").

He traces how the cause of her illness was discovered. ("Ms. Smith's illness was linked to the hamburger only by chance. Her aunt still had some of the frozen patties, and state health officials found that they were contaminated with a powerful strain of E. coli that was genetically identical to the pathogen that had sickened other Minnesotans.")

And he ends by circling back to where he began, with Smith herself.

> For Ms. Smith, the road ahead is challenging. She is living at her mother's home in Cold Spring, Minn. She spends a lot of her time in physical therapy, which is being paid for by Cargill in anticipation of a legal claim, according to Mr. Marler. Her kidneys are at a high risk of failure. She is struggling to regain some basic life skills and deal with the anger that sometimes envelops her. Despite her determination, doctors say, she will most likely never walk again.

Still, the piece ultimately focuses more broadly on food safety and not her illness and recovery. Moss offers a means of telling that complex story with maximum impact.

McCarthy, on the other hand, stays tightly focused on the single murder of seventeen-year-old Lance Zarders, not the broader issue of homicide in his city. In some ways, his approach entails an even bigger challenge. Long personal narratives work best when the physical or psychological challenge facing the story's central character gets resolved, warns Jon Franklin, in his book *Writing for Story*. "A story consists of a sequence of actions that occur when a sympathetic character encounters a complicating situation that he confronts and solves," he writes.[1]

But as he reported, McCarthy had no idea where his story would lead or whether the case would be solved. All he could do was accompany the detectives on the case, gather every detail and piece of evidence possible, and hope his story would prove compelling enough to justify all the time he was putting into reporting it and all the space the newspaper was committing to publishing it.

Such instantaneous *immersion* is truly a journalistic high-wire act, one with a high risk of failure. The two detectives McCarthy followed never did find Zarders's killer. Yet, even with, or perhaps because of, this ambivalent ending, McCarthy told the story with such intensity and skill that it earned him Columbia University School of Journalism's 2009 Berger Award for "the best in-depth human interest reporting" of the year.

As different as their stories are, certain aspects of the approaches taken by Moss and McCarthy are parallel. Both built their stories around an individual example that served as a universal for a bigger story. And both came full circle in their stories to where they had begun—Moss to Smith's paralysis, and McCarthy to the detectives being called out on yet another crime. The detectives had failed; now they would try again. Here is how McCarthy's series ended.

> (Detectives) Wischan and Pardo don't sleep well the night after their case tanked.

Wischan's name sits on top of the homicide division's Up List, so they'll get another killing to investigate any time now.

Sometime around 3 a.m., a man slits an acquaintance's throat in eastern New Orleans: Homicide 100. Within minutes, the detectives' cell phones ring.

As mentioned in chapter 3 ("Culling Life's Experience"), there's a name for this technique: *bookending*, or *circling back*. It means returning in some way to where the story began. It creates a symmetry to reading and writing that, as I get older, I realize may just be part of how we're wired, not merely as readers but also as humans.

Kathy and I, for example, met in the mountains of Colorado. Our first date was a camping trip. As we cleared out our garage for a sale in 2009, instead of selling camping equipment unused for more than a decade, we decided to head back to the woods. In summer 2009, I joined my high school class each fall and spring on a backpacking trip through the White Mountains of New Hampshire. The same summer, I found myself back on one of the same trails with friends. In the fall, Kathy and I returned to the Whites to watch the fall foliage.

If life's symmetry makes a certain sense as we get older—and I do hope my story doesn't end for awhile—story symmetry also gives readers a sense of closure, completeness, and final purpose as they read.

STRATEGIES FOR TELLING STORIES

This chapter will focus on several broad strategies for organizing stories. Its topic, story organization, could well be a book in itself. So I won't attempt to be exhaustive. Unlike some books dedicated to teaching feature writing, it won't lead you through a dozen or more story types with names such as "backgrounder," "profile," "news feature," and "brite." Instead, I'll talk about some of the simple, tested ways writers go from start to finish without losing their reader, their story, or their voice.

Listen to Tom Hallman, a Pulitzer Prize winner and master storyteller at the Portland *Oregonian*. Hallman is a soft-spoken and seemingly humble man, not too self-important, after all his writing prizes, to cover news, and always on the lookout for a little story that can convey a larger message. After he won an award for nondeadline writing from the American Society of Newspaper Editors, he said these words in an interview printed in the book *Best Newspaper Writing 1997*.

> I'm drawn to what I would call a pure story. . . . It's a story with a beginning, a middle, and an end. And I hope that my words draw readers through this story, that they learn something about the character, the life the character leads. And when they get to the end, I hope that I've changed the way they

look at the world or the way they look at people or the way they look at this person I've introduced them to.[2]

No matter how they're organized, stories need a beginning, a middle, and an end. In that beginning, writers must introduce the reader to the story's central character or characters, establish its central focus and, sometimes, set its context, establishing its place in the broader landscape of what's being written about the subject. In the middle, writers give muscle and flesh to the central theme's spine, providing detail and example that illuminate main points; connecting or *transitioning* between main themes or scenes; and moving forward logically and sequentially. In the end, writers need to reemphasize the main story line and either resolve it or reinforce its message, sometimes by circling back to a strong image, a surprise detail, or a summary quote. What endings should never do is belabor; preachers are not welcome.

Let's take these ideas one at a time.

THREE WAYS TO BEGIN

Straight Chronology

Readers are busy people. They need to be hooked to read on. So few stories start at the beginning and end at the end. Straight chronology can work, as it did for McCarthy's telling of New Orleans's "Homicide 37," if it immediately thrusts the reader into the story's action. With few exceptions (sections that look back at the victim's and suspect's past lives), he stayed with chronology over eight installments, establishing his story's backbone.

Chronology can work in smaller action-driven pieces as well. For example, on the twentieth anniversary of the 1989 Loma Prieta earthquake, I posted this remembrance on my blog, "Newsprints," at *True/Slant*:

> It was 14 seconds I'll never forget.
> Twenty years ago, I was sitting at the San Jose Mercury News city desk, revved up to coordinate the news coverage of Game 3 of the Bay Area World Series between the Oakland Athletics and San Francisco Giants. As pre-game coverage clicked on at 5 p.m. our reporters were in place. Four minutes later, the TV went silent and newsroom's concrete floor rippled like a ship's wake.
> We all dove. As I lay beneath my desk, legs protruding, I wondered whether the newsroom ceiling would collapse. The entire room rumbled, but I heard just one voice, that of another assistant city editor.
> "Oh my God," she said softly.
> And then the wave stopped.

Anecdote to Nut Graf

Sometimes called the "Wall Street Journal model" after the newspaper that perfected it, newspaper feature stories often start with the specific *anecdotal* or *scene-setter* lead, broaden to a more universal *nut graf*, and then eventually circle back to where they began. For such leads to work, several things are essential:

- The anecdote or descriptive scene has to reflect the story's central theme. The *New York Times'* Moss, for example, couldn't have started with Stephanie Smith's paralysis, if the story had been about a new way of inspecting food processing plants. Then, his dramatic lead would have deceived his readers.
- The anecdote has to fit the tone and content of the story. Writers shouldn't wrap direct, fact-based news reports in the window dressing of anecdote. Such a lead can deceive the reader by promising a more leisurely and personal story than the writer ultimately delivers.
- The writer can't waste words. These leads should never be an excuse for overwriting. Each subsequent sentence has to engage *and* add additional information. No adjective-laden fluff, please.
- An anecdote must be compelling. Not every vignette is worth telling.

The longer any lead stretches, the more work it must do. Each sentence must contain fresh detail, a reason to read on. Readers get impatient quickly. In newspapers and on the Web, anecdotal leads (or leads that set a physical scene) usually resolve in a clear nut graf three to five paragraphs into a story. In magazine writing, they sometimes dally a bit longer.

Here is an example from the *New York Times*, written by Isabel Wilkerson after the Mississippi River had flooded its banks. The nut graf is italicized.

> On a balmy Sunday after church, Elizabeth Crane stood in a parking lot trying to recall her address. It had been a month since the river took the house she lived in for 44 years, the little town of Hardin, Mo., where she settled as a war bride, the antique table linens from her mother in Germany and even the cemetery where she buried her husband.
>
> "Let me see," she said, looking to the pavement for clues. She thought hard, then opened her purse and began mining for anything with her house number on it, growing more frustrated with each wrong envelope she found.
>
> "Here it is," she said, finally, retrieving a scrap of paper. "Front Street. 402 Front Street."
>
> *The river that had broken her heart took a piece of her memory, too.*
>
> *It has been nearly three months since the great rivers rose up against towns and farms in the Midwest. In some places the rivers are rising again, and now—after weeks of levee-shoring heroism followed by the tearful*

taking of inventory and determined efforts to clean up—the signs of post-traumatic stress, the kind that haunts some combat veterans and survivors of plane crashes, have set in among many of the region's people.

Such journalistic stories, known as *features*, frequently highlight a *trend*, something new or different that doesn't announce itself as news but has growing currency in a culture. The brief anecdote here sets up a trend feature on the growth of V.I.P. tickets on the rock concert scene. Again, the nut grafs are italicized. The second one both establishes context and explains something of the "why" of the trend.

Hershey, Pa.—Helena Aguiar had come all the way from Sao Paulo, Brazil, for a front-row seat to see her favorite band, and she got it: a black metal folding chair with a gold and cherry-red BonJovi logo on the cushion, hers to take home. The price: $1,750.

"It was an amazing experience, even more than I dreamed," Ms. Aguiar, 25, gushed after the show at Hersheypark Stadium here on Wednesday night, as she packed up her chair and lugged it to a parking lot.

Nearly a decade after "The Producers" introduced the $480 ticket to Broadway, V.I.P. pricing has established itself in the ledgers of Rock n' roll. . . .

Once available only for top-dollar tours by the likes of U2 or the Rolling Stones, V.I.P. packages have trickled down to the rank-and-file of live music, as artists try to maximize grosses and reap some of the markup value that the best seats get on resale sites like StubHub.com.

—New York Times

Sometimes a story will use a series of short examples instead of a single anecdote that leads to a nut graf. That's what a team of Portland *Oregonian* reporters did to begin the third part of their series on immigration that won the 2001 Pulitzer Prize for Public Service reporting.

Luis Gonzalez was forced to leave the country when his son was eight weeks old, and didn't get home until his child was a walking, talking toddler of 3.

Antonio Hernandez has spent the past five months alone in Alaska, while his wife and kids are marooned in Mexico.

Rene Hamilton is 13 and faces the prospect of having to choose between his parents.

All are casualties of immigration law and policies that have torn apart families and blasted away at bedrock principles of the United States' treatment of newcomers.

"There's a whole bunch of people suffering," says Rene's father, Thomas Hamilton, 47, who fled Cuba 20 years ago and now stands to lose his wife and son. "Something is terribly wrong."

Family unity traditionally has been the foundation for U.S. immigration policy, which has welcomed spouses, children and parents of American citizens by granting them protected status in securing citizenship and other benefits.

But many now are locked up without due process of law or have been booted out of the country without so much as a hearing, breaking up families nationwide.

Establishing Dramatic Tension

Think of the calm before the storm, a technique action movies rely on time and time again. A father walks hand in hand to school with his daughter, talking lightheartedly about afternoon plans. Suddenly, masked gunmen surround them. A climber heads toward the summit under sunny skies. Soon the radio crackles with news of an avalanche. The sexy, muscle-bound guy convinces the smitten, innocent girl to make one stop on the way to college classes to pick up a package for him. As she pulls out of the UPS parking lot and drives off, another car pulls from the curb and follows.

The scene moves from calm to the hint of chaos. It establishes tension. And then the camera dissolves and the film flashes back to an earlier, safer, and happier time. We're dying to know what happened, but the answer won't come for another hour or two—until just before the movie's end.

In writing stories, establishing dramatic tension is often a bit subtler than in the movies. The circumstance complicating our main characters' lives may not be life threatening. The tension may be built around relationships or an inner struggle. It may be psychological rather than physical. Still, the idea is the same: the lead, as the movie's opening, is designed to *hook* the audience, to hint at what's to come, and interest readers in the character or characters at the heart of that complicating situation. (If we don't care about them, we won't keep reading. That's why Franklin, in *Writing for Story*, admonishes writers to find not merely a character to write about but one that is *sympathetic*, that readers will care about.) Just as in the movies, the resolution will come later, near the end.

The best narrative piques interest and establishes a story's direction but leaves the tension they've built unresolved. They give readers a reason for turning the page until the end. They are *not* news: front loaded, explicitly clear, and summarized to the point that only the reader wanting details rather than story keeps reading. Also, narrative leads do not provide explicit nut grafs that summarize the stories' main point and then concentrate on providing details, interior anecdotes, and examples that further prove that point. Their goal is to *hook*, to reel the reader further in.

Here is an example from the *Los Angeles Times* that began a powerful 2006 series, "Blighted Homeland," that exposed the devastating repercussions of uranium mining on the Navajo Nation homeland and the impact. It was written by Judy Pasternak.

Oljato, Utah — Mary and Billy Boy Holiday bought their one-room house from a medicine man in 1967. They gave him $50, a sheep and a canvas tent.

For the most part, they were happy with the purchase. Their Navajo hogan was situated well, between a desert mesa and the trading-post road. The eight-sided dwelling proved stout and snug, with walls of stone and wood, and a green-shingle roof.

The single drawback was the bare dirt underfoot. So three years after moving in, the Holidays jumped at the chance to get a real floor. A federally funded program would pay for installation if they bought the materials. The Holidays couldn't afford to, but the contractor, a friend of theirs, had an idea.

He would use sand and crushed rock that had washed down from an old uranium mine in the mesa, one of hundreds throughout the Navajo reservation that once supplied the nation's nuclear weapons program. The waste material wouldn't cost a cent. "He said it made good concrete," Mary Holiday recalled.

As promised, the 6-inch slab was so smooth that the Holidays could lay their mattresses directly on it and enjoy a good night's sleep.

They didn't know their fine new floor was radioactive.

What happened to the Holiday family? The answer comes later. But already the reader knows enough to worry—and to want to keep reading.

Narrative techniques can work atop some shorter stories, too. Here is an example from Donna Britt, a longtime, award-winning metro columnist for the *Washington Post*.

It's strange, remembering the drool when I have so many lovely mementos: A lacy black cocktail glove. A paste-tinted photo of a couple in 1930's dress. A gold watch with chains as delicate as blades of new grass.

But there's something obscene about me having my grandmother's things. They belong in Pennsylvania, on the mantelpiece of Mom-Mommy's stone-columned home, hidden beneath a drawerful of decades-old finery.

They don't belong in Maryland with me.

So last week, I started avoiding my keepsakes. But slipping off the watch didn't stop the memories I'd just as soon forget.

What do I know here? Something has happened to Britt's grandmother, something she can't easily forget. But just what, or how she resolves it, will wait, because this is where the lead ends. The next paragraph starts at the beginning: "The late-night call came three weeks ago, on my birthday." From there, her story moves forward chronologically.

MAKING SENSE OF THE MIDDLE

I first coached Mary Wiltenburg at the *Christian Science Monitor* when she was assigned to write a profile of a September 11 widow as that day of infamy's first anniversary approached. Even then, in her midtwenties, Wiltenburg challenged herself to see things, and write them, differently. She'd caught the eye of editors when she traveled to a Kentucky medium-security prison to tell the story about an inmate drama group that included murderers, rapists, and others convicted of serious crimes. Wiltenburg wrote the story in acts, focusing in large part on the self-discovery these hardened men achieved through drama.

Acts, chapters, themes, and chronology are but a few of the ways writers organize their stories after drawing readers' attention. As writers do so, they need to keep the following four points in mind.

Remember Why the Piece Matters

Every story builds from a single dominant point. The lead establishes it. The body can't afford to abandon it. Pasternak's series looked back at the shameful history of uranium mining on the Navajo reservation and its impact on the people living there. She didn't just start writing everything she had learned about uranium. When stories become encyclopedic, they lose interest as well as focus.

Remember the Writer Is in Charge

This sounds self-evident. But too often new writers forget they, and not their subjects, are the real storytellers. After sweating through their lead and pulling the reader in, they relinquish their responsibility, allowing the story to be told in rambling *quotations*, wide swaths of words exactly as they came from their subjects' mouths. While *quotes* can and should punctuate a story, making it colorful or vivid, they should not be its staple, its main ingredient. I tell my students that quotes are the story's salsa, not its chips. They add spice.

Wiltenburg, for example, joined two short, powerful quotes by Curt Tofteland, who directed the imprisoned Kentucky actors and who also had directed the Kentucky Shakespeare Festival, in this paragraph from her piece.

> "I let the guys choose their roles," he says, "and you'd be surprised how many choose to act out the very kinds of things they're in here for." The inmates have told him those roles allow them to grapple with emotions they wouldn't otherwise be able to confront safely. "I tell them, 'You choose your role, but your role also chooses you'—and I believe that happens for a reason."

Short, focused quotes, like the two here within quotation marks, allow the reader to hear voices other than the writer's. They don't, however, take the writer's place.

Seek Details and Examples That Show What the Story Tries to Tell

"Can you give me an example?" It's a question I probably ask more than any other in conducting an interview, because it is the examples of writing, the specific images, that engage readers.

When Senator Ted Kennedy died of brain cancer in 2009, *New York Times* reporter Mark Leibovich wrote a moving story that looked back at his final, private months. Sometimes journalistic storytelling follows the admonition "tell it, then tell it again." I prefer "tell it, then show what you've told with specific detail." That is what Leibovich's piece did, ending an eight-paragraph first section that summed up Kennedy's final days with the following words: "But interviews, with close friends and family members yield a portrait of a man who in his final months was at peace with the end of his life and grateful for the chance to savor the salty air and the company of loved ones."

It continued with examples such as this one:

> Starting in late July, Vicki Kennedy organized near-nightly dinner parties and singalongs at the Kennedy compound in Hyannis Port. The senator was surrounded in the dining room by his crystal sailing trophies and a semi-regular cast of family members that included his three children, two step-children and four grandchildren. Jean Kennedy Smith, Mr. Kennedy's sister, had rented a home down the street this summer and became a regular, too. Instead of singing, she would sometimes recite poetry.
>
> Even as Mr. Kennedy became frustrated about his limitations, friends say his spirit never flagged. "This is someone who had a fierce determination to live, but who was not afraid to die," said Representative Bill Delahunt, a Democrat and a Kennedy friend whose district includes Cape Cod. "And he was not afraid to have a lot of laughs until he got there."
>
> —*New York Times*

Convey Information within the Frame of Story

This is one of the hardest parts of writing, moving from idea to idea, from theme to theme, and from scene to scene without, on the one hand, losing the story's thread by including too much or, on the other, sacrificing detail important for understanding just to keep the story line simple. Not all stories can be told in a clear chronological path. Not all key points and scenes connect seamlessly. Yet, connect they must for readers to read on. These tips might help:

- When possible, write in chapters. They make it easier for the writer to organize and the reader to digest.
- Use time to your advantage. We organize our lives in hours, days, weeks, and months. Why not do the same, whenever possible, with the stories we tell?

- Use transitional language to tip your reader when you are changing course or direction.

Writing in Chapters

A former boss of mine at the *San Jose Mercury News*, now a college president, counseled his editors and reporters not to be intimidated by a story's scope. With longer stories, he told his staff, think in smaller bites. They make storytelling less imposing.

What he didn't say is that these smaller sections, or *chapters*, also help hold readers because each serves as a ministory within a longer piece. At best, each chapter has a lead that reengages readers and an ending that entices those readers to start the next section.

It's a technique Wiltenburg, the *Monitor* writer who told the story of the Kentucky inmate-actors, frequently tries to apply. "I look at (each chapter) in the same sense as I look at a story overall," Wiltenburg said. "Its first sentence absolutely has to make you want to read the second sentence, and the last sentence has to make you want to read the next section."

Wiltenburg used this approach in writing about Sue Mladenik, the Chicago suburban widow whose husband was among the ninety-two passengers killed when American Airlines Flight 11 crashed into the north World Trade Center tower on September 11, 2001. Wiltenburg not so much told as showed Mladenik's struggle to right her life while keeping her husband's memory alive and guarding herself and her children from the overwhelming publicity that followed that day. Wiltenburg's story relies heavily on her reporting, which chronicled details and internal vignettes that helped readers visualize and understand Mladenik's life. She also tries to use a story within the story—Mladenik's decision to adopt another child, both to honor her husband's memory and reaffirm her faith in family—to keep readers interested from start to finish.

Here is her entire story. Consider these questions as you read it. To what extent does Wiltenburg achieve her goals? Does the detail of her reporting help draw you to the place and characters? Does she create a ministory out of each chapter? Do the chapters fit together? And does she leave enough unresolved to draw readers through to the end?

SHE DOESN'T WANT TO SHARE HER GRIEF WITH A NATION

Hinsdale, Ill.—It took her five days to leave her bedroom, ten months to wash the sheets they'd slept in together, and more than a year to empty the dirty socks from Jeff's gym bag.

But it didn't take Sue Mladenik long to get that fence up.

Cont.

Last Sept. 11, when her husband boarded American Airlines Flight 11 for a short, ugly trip, Sue and her four children became instant celebrities in their Chicago suburb. As the World Trade Center towers burned on TV, and word that Jeff might have been on that first plane spread up and down Hinsdale's maple-lined avenues, neighbors flocked to the Mladeniks' house. Reporters blocked their driveway. Churches took up collections.

A woman Sue hardly knew wept and clung to her at the post office. Sue walked out without mailing her package. "I don't need to cry with strangers," she says.

Far from the scarred earth and public shrines, the Mladeniks had become a living link to a day that—the TV anchors promised—would Change America Forever.

Sue hated it—hated not only the fact of her family's devastation, but its publicness.

The way everybody suddenly seemed to know her. The way Jeff died daily on the covers of newspapers and magazines.

She hated the fact that her 4-year-old understood enough to ask: "Was Dada on the first or second plane?" And she hated suspecting that some of the "old friends" on her doorstep were only after a piece of her big-news grief.

"Sure, our friends wanted to be there for us," she says. "But then there are those other people, the people who came out of the woodwork."

So Sue ringed the backyard with a six-foot fence. Behind it, she thought, she might grieve in peace. She wanted to quit being "the local freak show." She wanted to sit like any other mom and watch her daughter swing.

For the moment, money wasn't a pressing concern: Mortgage insurance had paid off her house, and the life insurance policy at the Web publishing company Jeff headed had been a good one. Sue knew she'd have to go back to work eventually, but she wasn't in a hurry. Still, she worried. Her daughter, Kelly, 22, had moved back home after Jeff's death and was struggling with substance abuse. Josh, 19, was quietly grinding his teeth at night. Seventeen-year-old Daniel said he couldn't stand being with Sue, "because all you do is cry." Gracie, the youngest, wouldn't let Sue out of her sight.

Sue had always relied on Jeff for discipline. She didn't see how she could raise four children alone. But more than ever, they were the reason she got out of bed: her purpose and her sustenance.

As the days passed, her thoughts turned to a fifth child, waiting in a Chinese orphanage, for whom she and Jeff had chosen the name Hannah.

It's not just her wedding ring. These days, wherever she goes, Sue also wears two silver bracelets engraved with her husband's name and flight number, a WWJD bracelet ("This is probably blasphemy," she says, "but to me it stands for
Cont.

'What would Jeff do?'"), a replica of her husband's class ring on a chain, a gold heart pendant with a hologram of his face, a twin towers pin, and a heart pin with a hole in it.

Jeff's best friend, Tad Lagastee, jokes that she's turning into a walking shrine.

But at the strip malls on the edge of her town of 17,000, the jewelry doesn't set her apart. People say the heart is cute. A Wal-Mart checker recently asked if the face on her necklace was The King.

Sue looked at her blankly.

"You know, Elvis?" the checker said.

Jeff and Sue grew up around here. They met after high school, working at the mall, and married when they were 20 and 21. For several years, Jeff's marketing jobs kept the family moving: to Florida, to Arizona. When they moved back to Illinois in the early '90s with three small children, they were ready to land somewhere.

After Daniel went to kindergarten, Sue got a job teaching preschool. She was a great teacher, partner Mary Seiferth remembers. "But Sue was always a mother first. A fierce mother."

In 1996, Jeff and Sue watched a TV exposé on Chinese orphanages. The squalor and deprivation lingered in their minds; Jeff started looking into international adoptions. A year later, Sue quit teaching, and in 1998 the couple traveled to the Linchuan Social Welfare Institute to bring Gracie home. Last summer, they filed paperwork to begin the adoption process again, and chose a name for their daughter-to-be.

But by early fall, Sue was a grieving single mother of four. Hannah's dossier was no longer valid. Sue had to make a choice.

"People ask me, 'What were you thinking?' but there was nothing that was going to keep me from this child," she says. "I know it's what Jeff would have expected of me."

Facing the specter of a second loss, Sue furiously refiled her paperwork. And waited.

The grief comes in waves. She'll be having a perfectly normal day, and suddenly Sue will be blind-sided by it. "I've had to leave stores. I'll be in the grocery and it'll be his favorite cookie or something and suddenly I'm crying."

When she closes her eyes, she sees Jeff's last minutes alive. Most nights she sleeps only a few hours. In shops, in parking lots, when women complain about their husbands, snip at them for this or that, she wants to shake them: "Lady, stop it. He could be gone like that!"

Sue and Jeff hardly ever fought. Family friends say they were always struck— even when he was working long hours and the kids were running her ragged—by how much in love the pair seemed.

Though Jeff traveled a lot for work, especially in his last job as interim CEO of the Web publisher eLogic, he didn't enjoy it.

Cont.

Every night, he'd call Sue. They'd chat about their days, the kids, and what they would do together that weekend. Then he'd say, "I love you, sweetheart." And she'd answer, the way she did that last night, "I love you too. Talk to you tomorrow."

She couldn't sleep until she had heard from him.

His death gave her more to lie awake worrying about: insurance benefits, DNA samples, television executives' tasteless decisions.

In March, she heard CBS was planning to air new footage of Jeff's crash. Sue appealed to her China adoption e-mail lists; friends and sympathizers sent the network hundreds of protest letters.

"Sensationalizing the murder of my husband and thousands of other innocent victims is shameful," Sue wrote to CBS executive Gil Schwartz. "You have no idea what my life, or the lives of our children is like EVERY single day."

"You know when someone gets married they say the two shall become one? Well, I am no longer one."

Some days, Sue says, she feels she hardly resembles the person she was a year ago. "I look at our government differently now, I look at low-flying planes differently now." She and Gracie don't go to the zoo anymore; they see too many "mommy-daddy happy families" there.

It bothers her particularly not to have her husband's body to bury. Though workers recovered a bone fragment matching Jeff's DNA, it's little comfort. Sue wants to put a stone at his head, to visit him, to mourn him on her own terms, "but I could bury him in a shoebox right now."

Some say every American is a Sept. 11 victim. Sue doesn't buy it.

If everybody grieved when the towers fell, why do they use the same tired lines on her they've always used? How can they say, "You'll find someone else"? Or, "He's in a better place"?

"I don't think he's in a better place," she says. "There is no better place. You might as well kick me in the stomach."

She knows Jeff wouldn't be proud of her anger. He believed in heaven. At Christ Church of Oak Brook, the 5,000-member evangelical congregation he was drawn to for its seriousness about the Gospel, he taught a class for newlyweds. His last lessons were about humbling yourself before God.

"I'm just not there yet," she says. "I don't believe there's a better place for him than, selfishly, with me. But mostly with my children."

Her children have always been the center of Sue's life—sometimes, friends say, to a fault. Sue says they're the reason she's still alive.

But Jeff's friend Tad, now one of Sue's closest confidants too, says her single-minded family focus is more than a distraction from grief. "I think Sue sees loving her family as her way to love Jeff," he says. "Call it therapy, call it a love affair. Call it what you want: He was her sweetheart."

Cont.

In some ways, Sue says, losing Jeff on Sept. 11 was probably a lot like what it would have been to lose him any other day. That same impossible feeling of: "I can't believe this is my life. I can't believe this is the rest of my life."

"The difference," she says, "is not many people get to see their loved one blown to bits over and over on TV."

And not many people's losses are celebrated as "anniversaries."

"I still can't quite spit out 'anniversary,'" says Sue, "because anniversaries are happy things. They're things you celebrate. They're things Jeff and I celebrated."

She wants to mark the day, though. This Sept. 11, Sue hopes to take her kids to ground zero, to hear the names of the victims read, and to meet the wife of the man who sat next to her husband in his final minutes.

But she won't have much time to spend looking back. This March, after months of waiting, Sue got Hannah's adoption referral in the mail.

Two weeks ago, despite Daniel's promise never to fly again, the family boarded a plane to Beijing. Last Sunday, they held 1-year-old Hannah for the first time.

On Thursday, Sue plans to bring all five children home to Hinsdale.

There, in the crib by Sue's bed, a pile of teddy bears made from Jeff's favorite shirts is waiting. "I hate that Hannah will never know her father—at least in this world," she says.

"But she'll know what kind of man he was, and she'll know he loved her. I'll make sure."

—*by Mary Wiltenburg*

In her story, Wiltenburg conveys Mladenik's dignity, a hint of bitterness, and her fierce devotion to her children and to her husband. In her reporting, she mines the details that infuse emotion without stating it in a heavy-handed way (see chapter 10, "Bring Back the Breed of the Dog," for more on reporting). It's there from the teddy bears made "from Jeff's favorite shirts" to the dirty socks she had yet to take, a year later, from his gym bag. What other details in the story help develop Mladenik and her character? Are there details you'd like to see that are missing?

Interspersing Narrative and Exposition

Some stories are more complex. They don't allow the writer to stay with a single subject from start to finish. They demand historical context, draw on more than one main character, and require explanation that falls outside the narrative's realm.

In wrestling with such complexity, writers sometimes move back and forth between pure narrative and more expository sections or chapters. Pasternak did just that in telling her story of the poisoning of Navajo lands. She began the series "Blighted Homeland" with the lead about Mary and Billy Boy Holiday's radioactive floor.

Throughout the first installment of this four-part series, which won the 2007 James V. Risser reporting prize, she interweaves the story of the Holidays and their extended family with that of broader tragedy that befell their Navajo community. Here's an excerpt that shows the way Pasternak moves back and forth from family to the history and neglect that caused their suffering:

Not until 2000 did the Holidays learn that their hogan was dangerous. By then, the couple had raised three children and sheltered a host of other kin while the uranium decayed. The resulting alpha, beta and gamma rays were invisible; the radon gas was odorless. But the combination greatly increased the chance of developing fatal lung cancer, according to a radiation expert who sampled air in the hogan.

"It brings chills when you're told that your house is like this," said Mary Holiday, now in her early 70s. "All the years that you've lived here," she said, her voice trailing off.

Unsuspecting, she had gone about her chores in the Navajo way, clad in the customary velveteen blouse, long skirt, thick socks and dusty shoes. She chopped wood for the stove, cooked tortillas and brewed tea. She set up her loom to weave rugs under a juniper tree while the grandchildren played dress-up for hours inside the old hogan.

By the time of the discovery that now torments her, she had lost her husband, Billy Boy, to lung cancer and congestive heart failure. He didn't smoke, but he'd worked in uranium mines by day and slept, unknowing, in the equivalent by night.

Her grandnephew, too, would soon die of lung cancer, at age 42. He had neither smoked nor mined. But he had lived in the hogan for three years as a teenager.

The dwellings in the Holiday family compound faced east toward dawn, in accordance with Navajo tradition. Behind them loomed the mesa, with a pale green uranium stain that started at the old mine and pointed down the cliff.

"Where Is Our Guardian?"

More than 180,000 people live scattered across the region bounded by the Navajos' four sacred peaks. More than a homeland, it is their holy land. The tribe's creation stories are set here, among the painted deserts, ponderosa highlands and layered sandstone cliffs.

The U.S. government appealed to both Navajo patriotism and self-interest when it asked the tribe to open its land to uranium exploration in the 1940s. The mining would aid the American war effort and provide jobs, federal officials said.

Some of the mining companies were conglomerates like Kerr-McGee Corp. Some were small like A&B Mining, a Utah firm that was the last to mine the mesa near the Holidays' hogan.

Early on, federal scientists knew that mine workers were at heightened risk for developing lung cancer and other serious respiratory diseases in 15 or 20 years. Many did, and eventually their plight drew wide attention. In 1990, Congress offered the former miners an apology and compensation of up to $150,000 each.

But pervasive environmental hazards remained.

—*Los Angeles Times*

The piece, of course, returns to the Holidays several more times, ending with the death of that grand-nephew, mentioned above.

Using Time to Your Advantage

From my experience as editor and coach, writers sometimes make storytelling more complicated than need be. Stories unfold most naturally in chronological order. Sure, the writer must first hook the reader. But then it works just fine to start at the beginning and go to the end.

This isn't a license for long-windedness. All writing needs to separate wheat from chaff. Writers should never dally simply to self-indulge. That said, time is the best natural transition that exists. We're driven by it. We know 5:00 p.m. precedes 6:00 p.m. and yesterday came before today. Why turn things inside out?

In the second chapter of her 9/11 widow, Wiltenburg relied on chronology to show the love affair that was their life together. She also used chronology at various points in her yearlong *Christian Science Monitor* series on "Little Bill Clinton: A School Year in the Life of a New American," which chronicled the story of a boy, Bill Clinton Hadam, and his refugee family's struggles after their relocation to Georgia.

Many of her stories were her near-daily blogs, one of which told of a run-in that Bill's Rwandan-born mother, Dawami Lenguyanga, had with the American legal system because of misunderstandings of language, culture, and custom. This story, about a day in court, sets the scene, and then proceeds chronologically, saving the resolution, and punch line, for last. It is unusual, although increasingly less so, in that it appeared first as a blog and then was adapted into a newspaper story. Its informal tone, more letter than reported story, and its slightly editorialized ending reflect the intimacy that makes storytelling on the blogosphere somewhat different and more personal than at most print outlets. However, its main point—that refugees trip regularly over a culture of misunderstanding—couldn't be more clear.

Atlanta

Tuesday afternoon, Rwandan Dawami Lenguyanga stood before an annoyed Judge Catherine Malicki of the Municipal Court of Atlanta for her arraignment on a charge of disorderly conduct. As Dawami's friend Felix Mulamba translated, and her co-worker Felicia Jackson tried to testify on Dawami's behalf, the judge frowned over her glasses.

"I don't have time [for this]," she snapped.

Dawami's latest encounter with the American legal system (earlier, an arrest warrant had been issued after she misunderstood a traffic court summons, costing her $340) began late one night last month when she tried to catch the subway home from work. She and Felicia, a Liberian refugee who came to Atlanta three years ago and has been doing housekeeping at Georgia State University two months longer than Dawami, bought fare cards and swiped them at the entrance of MARTA, the local transit system. A man stood on the platform, watching them.

Felicia's card worked fine, but when Dawami scanned hers, the women say, the card-reader couldn't register it. They were running to catch the train, which connected to the 10:45 p.m. bus home; if they missed it, [her two sons] Bill and Igey would be alone while they waited for the next one, at 12:15 a.m. So when Dawami's card failed to read, she piled through the gate behind Felicia and the women ran for their train.

The man, they say, followed them, shouting: "Put your hands behind your back!" Dawami—a native Swahili speaker who came to Atlanta two years ago—didn't understand the command. Felicia, a no-nonsense mother of five, intervened, explaining that Dawami didn't know much English. The man, a MARTA policeman, handcuffed Dawami and took her into a back room. Felicia says she waited nearly two hours for her friend's release, frantically showing the ticket saleswomen Dawami's receipt and fare card. She says that one ran the card through her machine, and confirmed that, as the receipt showed, it had $5 on it.

The MARTA officer, unnamed on the ticket, wrote this report: "Enter[ed] into the paid area without paying the required $1.75 fare by following a paying patron through the faregate"—and ordered Dawami to appear in court on a "disorderly conduct" charge.

There she was on Tuesday afternoon, missing work her first month on the job and baffled by prosecutor William Wansker's explanation of possible pleas: guilty, not guilty, and no contest. As he detailed the differences, Felix and Felicia conferred in French. Twice, Mr. Wansker asked them not to talk during his instructions. Then he took questions.

Hearing Dawami's charge on what he called a "DC-Section 5 fraudulent scheme," and realizing that she spoke little English, he recommended her for a "pretrial release" program through which she could return to court and get the charge dismissed by performing community service.

Felix, a naturalized US citizen from Congo, advised her to plead guilty and pay the fine, so she wouldn't miss more work. Felicia argued that Dawami didn't deserve to have a crime on her record—but said she couldn't afford to take off work again to come back and testify at a trial.

Dawami was torn between her belief in her innocence and her fear of losing a job it had taken a year to get. She needs to keep it if she hopes to be eligible to bring her daughter, Neema, to the US from Tanzania, where the family spent 10 years as refugees.

"I need to finish today," Dawami said. "If I come back, I lose work." She settled on a no-contest plea: She'd pay a fine, and the charge would remain on her record, but she wouldn't miss work again.

When Dawami's name was called—"Ms. Lenawhanga?" the judge tried— she, Felix, and Felicia approached a microphone.

"Judge there's a language issue here," the prosecutor warned. Judge Malicki asked how Dawami pled. No contest, said Felix.

According to court procedure, that should've been it. But Felicia had missed that instruction. Animated and indignant, she launched into her account of the incident.

The judge cut in, asking who the three were, which of them were charged, and whether they were related. She got quickly frustrated.

"Who's Dawami?" she asked. "Are y'all here to interpret? What language does she speak? Does she want a lawyer, sir?"

Felix conferred with Dawami. No, he replied, Dawami did not want a lawyer. The judge overruled them: "We're gonna put her down for not guilty, and I'm gonna recommend her for a public defender, and she will need to come back."

Felix started to protest that they couldn't miss work to return to court, when the prosecutor hailed me. He'd seen me sitting with them before the trial, and called me up to join them. "Can you help?"

"Who are you?" asked the judge incredulously. I said I was a reporter following Dawami's family for the year.

At that, the prosecutor hustled the four of us into a side room and asked us to explain what had happened, while the judge moved on to other traffic infractions.

Felicia, her fringed turban flapping, launched passionately into the story in her accented English. Felix advocated paying a fine and getting it over with. Dawami looked silently from one to the other to the bearded prosecutor.

"This is too murky for me," said Wansker. Felicia tried to show him the fare card and receipt. He gestured for her to keep them.

"Good enough," he said hurriedly. He was needed in the courtroom where 10 more defendants waited in line. "You know what? Dismissed. Dismissed." He wiped his hands together, to be sure the Africans understood.

They thanked him.

"These people don't have a clue," he commiserated to me as we reentered the courtroom.

Outside, the group hugged, and Felicia tore the ticket to shreds. "I'm so mad at that policeman," she said, "I say: 'Let me testify, even [if] I'm late to work.'"

As I drove the women to work to finish their shift, they and Felix talked about American racism and anti-immigrant bias. About the white MARTA cop who could've just explained to the newly arrived African what to do in case of a demagnetized fare card—but chose instead to handcuff her. About the court officials who treated them with impatience until my white face, fluent English, and press credentials stood beside them.

It's true: They don't fully understand the arraignment process.

There's a lot about America they still don't know. But they have a clue.

Transitions

Readers sometimes need turn signals to move from one idea to the next. These *transitions* can play a central role in organizing the midsection of any story. The best transitions are natural. One sentence follows the next. The flow is seamless. Sometimes, however, writers have to skip ahead or back in time, cross a room or a city, contrast what one speaker says with the words of another. When a story's road is no longer straight, the writer needs to provide those signs that steer the reader to the next passage. Sentences without them are like roads with no lanes or with unmarked intersections. Someone trying to navigate them is going to get off course, if not injured.

Typically, the "road signs" of writing—transitions—start the sentence that follows. Sometimes, they are tucked after the first few words or phrase. A road sign can be as simple as introducing new people as they enter a room or putting the identification and attribution of a speaker at the start of a sentence or quote to make clear someone different from the sentence before is speaking.

Let's move for the moment from that Atlanta refugee resettlement back to the countryside of Provence (this is a transitional sentence). *From the outset* (time *transition*), we were struck by the contrast between American stereotypes of France as a country of arrogant snobs and the droll and charming day-to-day interactions we had with the people who lived there. I wrote about this in an opinion piece for the *Christian Science Monitor* titled "The French Connection." *In the excerpt below* (place transition), the transitional words are italicized and qualified by type.

Next to nothing in our experience in France jibes with the stereotype of vaguely amusing, largely annoying, mirror-absorbed Frenchmen. OK, we had to deal once with a surly cab driver who tried to jack the price of a ride to our apartment. *But* [contrast transition] I've faced worse in Boston. *Other than that* [qualifying transition], Kathy and I have encountered no arrogance, no fussiness, no snobbery.

Instead [contrast transition], everywhere we turn, people greet us with a smile and a "Bonjour, monsieur et madame." Goodbyes are more elaborate— "Merci beaucoup; au revoir," and then, "bonne journee" or "bon weekend." People wait patiently while we mangle their language. *Often* [qualifying transition], in a most cordial way, they'll then correct our mistakes in French. It's the best way to learn.

We've seen the warmth and kindness of the Provencal French in the old-timer who stopped my cousin Jim outside a bakery to tell him that his shoe was untied, the bartender who ran after us to give us free postcards, the desk clerk in Villefranche-sur-Mer who drew us a color-coded map of the area's beach-front trails.

We've seen the humor in the waitress in the sleepy Mediterranean village of Les Saintes Marie de la Mer who served us an ample and divine meal of fish soup and daube (a Provençal stew of sorts) *after* [time transition] joking about the small but critical distinction between *le poisson* (fish) pronounced with an "s" sound, and *le poison* (poison), pronounced with a "z."

"If I served you poison," she said with a twinkle, "you would be dead."

We've seen their generosity, too. [transitional sentence]

The ruddy-faced non-nonsense manager of Joseph's bakery wrapped two apple turnovers in a bag for me, no charge, when Kathy returned to the States for two weeks, leaving me to fend for myself.

And the rugged cashier in the Provençal Alps allowed me to walk out of his ski rental shop with skis, boots, and poles and no paper trail other than my name. He'd taken no credit card imprint, requested no e-mail or phone number. *When I returned three days later* [time transition] and handed him 75 euros—the posted rate for the rental was 22 euros a day, almost $30—he handed me back 20 euros. He had asked for 59 euros. *But* [contrast transition] when I, confused, gave him too much, he decided to settle for 55. Can you imagine similar treatment at a US resort?

Here are some of the transitional words and phrases often used in writing.

PLACE TRANSITIONS

These examples note a change in location: *across the street, on the corner, upstairs, in Paris,* and *nearby.*

TIME TRANSITIONS

These help bridge a gap or change in time: *yesterday, later, then, afterward, the next week,* and *a few months later.*

CONTRASTS

I've noted some already. Other examples include: *however, despite, on the other hand,* and *nevertheless.*

LOGICAL TRANSITIONS

These examples draw a relationship between two ideas: *therefore, consequently, so,* and *because.*

ENDING STRONG

"Great lead," reporters sometimes say to compliment a colleague. Rarely does one hear, "Great ending." And yet it is the ending or *kicker* that stays with the reader longest, that final image or final thought the reader is left to digest.

"Endings," writes Carl Sessions Stepp in *Writing as Craft and Magic,* "provide resolution for the enduring reader, a sense of shared completion."[3] And yet lots of stories—in newspapers, magazines, books, and movies—start lively with the promise of great opening scenes only to stagger toward a close. They disappoint, leaving the audience feeling a bit cheated. Think about it. I'll bet you can recall a lot more riveting opening scenes to stories, books, and movies than you can recall closing scenes, which suggests that endings can be awfully tough to pull off. And yet, the work of art or craft that disappoints at the end, in some way disappoints overall, no matter how compelling the information or story up to that point.

Like most writers, Mary Wiltenburg starts her writing process by crafting her opening. She lays down scattered notes and scenes beneath it, but ignores them while she crafts her lead. Then she jumps to her story's ending, working on it, she says, until it has been stripped of false emotion and overwriting. She recalled her struggle in telling the story of Neema John, half-sister of Little Bill Hadam and daughter of Dawami (perhaps because of the intimacy of this series and because much of it rolled out as blog posts, Wiltenburg referred to her subjects by first name, an approach normally avoided in journalistic writing). When the family emigrated, she was left behind in Tanzania, which is where Wiltenburg visited her. For Wiltenburg, who wrote the story near the end of her year shadowing the family, it was perhaps the most difficult piece to write. To me, it was perhaps the most powerful to read, in part because of its ending.

Neema has led a brutal life. She watched at age seven as men shot and killed her father. She's been a refugee since. She was raped as a young teen, fled her parents' home in shame despite their entreaties, was raped again, had a son, and when two years later she returned to her parents' home, found they had gone to America. When Wiltenburg caught up with Neema, she was anxiously waiting for clearance to join her family in the United States before her twenty-first birthday, when the rules of entry would get much harder.

The opening scene of the story, "A Genocide Survivor Races the Clock to Get to the US," shows Neema trying to protect her son, something she has struggled to do for herself since childhood. The nut graf is italicized.

Dar es Salaam, Tanzania—She's learned to sleep in the rain. When spring storms pound the sheet-metal roof like a timpani and drip through marble-sized holes over the bed, Neema John curls around her son, Toni. Shifting the 4-year-old clear of the leaks, she rearranges the mosquito net around them and whispers until he drifts off again.

The 20-year-old has made the room where they live, in the Kigogo slum here, as cozy as she can. The bed, with its embroidered sheet, is made with hospital precision. Each brown couch cushion is topped with a teal doily. In one corner, a week's water sits in lidded five-gallon buckets; in another, a small clay stove stands ready.

In this neighborhood built on a trash heap, Neema is a world away from her little brothers, Bill Clinton Hadam and Igey Muzeleya. Resettled outside Atlanta two years ago as refugees, the boys have been attending US public schools, developing a taste for pizza and chicken fingers, and learning the names of TV wrestlers.

Their sister is a warm young woman with a ready smile. She's easy to love, and her neighbors do: Mama Suzy, across the hall, considers her a close friend; Oscar, a skinny teen next door, calls her his big sister. Neema's fond of them, too, but they don't really know her, she says. If she told them the truth, she could be deported, or worse: "There's no one here I can trust. If they found out what I really am, I don't know what they'd do."

What is Neema really? A victim and a survivor, a mother and a child. A stateless migrant, buffeted by the political and social violence that has swept Central Africa since she was a child.

The story progresses chronologically through Neema's life as a refugee, one of fourteen million worldwide. She is always running, always vigilant, often hurt. It ends by subtly bookending with the opening theme, returning to mother and son together in their slum dwelling, trying to make a home while waiting anxiously for word from America.

As dark fell on Kigogo one recent rainy evening and Neema lit the candle on the table, Toni came into the room crying. He didn't want to go to sleep. He wanted to leave with some young friends who'd been visiting from another part of the city.

From where she sat on the bed, Neema scooped him up. He stood on the bed frame in the candlelight, leaning into her.

"Aye, Toni. Ah, my baby boy." She nuzzled him with his favorite toy, a hand-me-down from Uncle Igey. "You want to leave Mama? [And] Doggy?"

"I want to go," he wept.

"You want to leave your room and go? No," she soothed, pawing him with the dog and softly woofing.

Outside, his friends shrieked, playing in the dark. On the stoop next door, women gossiped under a bare bulb. Up the hill in the square, vendors were erecting small tables with cold beer and hot barbecue. Faintly, the sound of a radio carried across the slum. Toni was choking on his tears. He wanted to leave—for good: "Mama, we'll go together."

Now Neema was battling tears, too: "Don't you remember yesterday, I showed you a plane?"

"No," he whimpered. But she had his attention.

"The one that passed over there?" She pointed over their heads, through the window grate.

"We're going to get on it and go to Grandma," she said. "Soon. Very soon."

The scene, Wiltenburg says, "kept coming back to me. It seemed to me where to end." She worried, however, about overwriting, about "getting gucky." And so she pared some more (see chapter 14, "No One Gets It Right the First Time").

"I work on [the ending] until it makes me cry," Wiltenburg says, only half-joking. "Not necessarily because it's sad or schmaltzy, but because it gets something so exactly. More than anything else in a story I think [the ending] has to be true to the people in it."

Wiltenburg's ending here worked at two levels: It recapitulated the emotion of the opening scene, of Neema's effort to keep her son safe. It also looked ahead, another effective way to conclude a story.

"Something I often do in my writing is to bring the story full circle," writes author William Zinsser, in *On Writing Well*, "to strike at the end an echo of a note that was sounded at the beginning. It gratifies my sense of symmetry, and it also pleases the reader, completing with its resonance the journey we set out on together."[4]

The best endings have one other quality. They don't belabor a point. They don't waste words. If anything, they end more abruptly than the reader expects.

It's time, once again, for you to write.

At the end of chapter 9, you interviewed a family member or friend about a moment or event that changed her or his life or perspective. In chapter 10, you interviewed others familiar with the story and drafted a single scene. Now try drafting the entire story. Ask yourself these questions:

1. How should I begin?

    Do I want to set a scene, as Mary Wiltenburg does at the start of her story about Neema John?

    Do I prefer to start with a short, powerful anecdote, like Michael Moss does with his story at the beginning of this chapter? Or do I want to try something else?

    Does this story call for a nut graf, something that anchors where the piece is heading and helps focus readers? Or do I want the opening to lure the reader in by hinting at, or foreshadowing, what's to come, as did Donna Britt in the essay about her grandmother?

2. Once I've hooked my reader, where will the story go?

    Does it lend itself to chronological progression?

    What scenes do I want to include?

    What transitions do I need, either within scenes or between them, for the story to flow smoothly?

    Might the story best be told in chapters? If so, how can I build tension into the start and conclusion of each?

    Is there expository information that should be broken out into separate chapters?

3. Where might the story end?

    Is there a dominant image that brings the story full circle?

    Is there a complicating event or circumstance that in some way your character resolves?

    Does the story lend itself to looking forward to the future?

Once you've answered these questions, write a headline, block key points in a brief outline, and then draft.

Fourteen
No One Gets It Right the First Time

The difference between the almost right word and the right word is really a large matter—it's the difference between the lightning bug and the lightning.

—Mark Twain[1]

The best writers tinker to the last second. This process doesn't shackle. It liberates, freeing writers from the quest for perfection at first keystroke. It enables, no, encourages writers to step away, clear cobwebs, and return refreshed, better prepared to pare the unnecessary and shape more pointed sentences.

For the deadline reporter, typing feverishly to turn a breaking news story, revision sometimes falls to editors who themselves are squeezed for time. For storytellers, whether professionals or amateurs, whether writing for a high-end magazine or a low-impact personal blog, the chance to redraft is a gift worth savoring.

Perhaps you're not convinced. Perhaps you believe revising squelches spontaneity, kills conversational cadence, drains energy, and saps voice. Forgive me, but you're wrong. Just as fast drafters dodge the self-doubt that all on the page is dreck (gaining, as Carl Sessions Stepp writes, confidence that breeds competence), writers who revise come closer to meeting William Strunk and E. B. White's challenge in the *Elements of Style*—to "make every word tell."[2] In doing so, they enhance their voice, that sense of effortless and engaged warmth the best writers impart even as, behind the scenes, they sweat unneeded words, sharpen scenes, and hew more closely to the story's course.

Donald Fry, a scholar and former dean turned journalism writing coach, has defined voice as "the sum of all the strategies used by the author to create the illusion that the writer is speaking directly to the reader from the page."[3] Each individual's strategies will vary. The path to polishing them remains constant: revising.

Let's track the changes in the first draft of this chapter's opening paragraphs. Here is that first draft, with the changes. Deleted words have a strike through them, and additions are italicized and in bold face.

First Draft

The ~~very~~ best writers tinker ~~with their work~~ up to the last second. This process ~~of revision~~ doesn't shackle. It liberates, freeing ~~the~~ writer**s** from the ~~burden of straining for~~ ***quest for*** perfection at first keystroke. ***It enables, no, encourages writers*** ~~Revising allows the writer~~ to step away ~~from her work~~, clear ***cobwebs,*** ~~her head~~ and return ~~with fresh eyes and renewed imagination. It leads to~~ ***refreshed, better prepared to pare the unnecessary and shape more pointed sentences.*** ~~stronger verbs, more precise word choice, and leaner sentences.~~

For the deadline reporter, typing feverishly to turn a breaking news story ~~on deadline~~, revision sometimes falls to ~~multiple levels of~~ editors who themselves are ~~under the gun~~ ***squeezed for time.*** For storytellers, whether ~~they write professionally or as a hobby~~ ***professionals or amateurs, whether writing*** for a high-end magazine or a ***low-impact*** personal blog, ~~redrafting, not once but several times over, is a luxury worth hording for themselves.~~ ***the chance to redraft is a gift worth savoring.***

Perhaps you're not convinced. Perhaps you believe revising squelches spontaneity, kills conversational cadence, ~~squeezes energy from a story,~~ even ***drains energy,*** saps ~~its~~ voice. ~~What can I say: You're~~ ***Forgive me, but you're*** wrong. Just as ~~the~~ fast drafter**s** ~~dodges~~ the self-doubt that all ***on the page*** is dreck (~~and thus retains~~ ***gaining,*** as Carl Sessions Stepp ~~would put it,~~ ***writes,*** ~~the~~ confidence ~~to build~~ ***that breeds*** competence), ~~the~~ writer**s** who revise**s** ***come closer to meeting William Strunk and E. B. White's challenge in the*** ~~reimposes discipline, strives to achieve the admonition of the authors of~~ *Elements of Style*—to "make every word tell." In doing so, the**y** ~~best~~ enhance their voice, the sense of effortless~~ness~~ ***and engaged warmth*** the best writers impart ***even as, behind the scenes, they sweat*** ~~as they shed the last~~ unneeded words, sharpen ~~their~~ scenes, and hew more closely to the story's course.

Notice that some words are more readily expendable than others. These include the following:

1. *Prepositional phrases.* In the first sentence, for example, I eliminated the words, "with their work." The preposition that begins the phrase here is "with." The two words that follow add little because with what else would writers tinker? Presumably, if they were tinkering with car engines, the sentence would specify. Look for prepositions,

those little words such as "for," "by," "of," and "from." They, and the words that immediately follow, are typically expendable.

2. *Fillers.* Words such as "very" and "even" are the writer's equivalent of a hitch in the batter's swing or a big, slow windup in the pitcher's delivery. Eliminate them.

3. *Passive verbs.* Sentence structure also matters. Sentences cast in the passive voice, in which the subject, instead of doing the acting, is acted on, are less clear and wordier.

Take the phrase "the germs were killed." It is passive. It doesn't tell me who or what killed them. Add "by antibiotics," and the writer has answered that question. But why not write, "Antibiotics killed the germs"? It is tighter, is more direct, and starts with the subject, the actor. That makes its voice active. Here is another example that is both less specific and wordier. "The destination was reached by bike in two hours." This nine-word sentence is again passive. It lacks vitality because it is vague. Let's change it to an eight-word sentence: "The children biked to the camp in two hours." This active version gives more information in less space. The sentence gains vitality.

TIPS FROM ROY PETER CLARK

Roy Peter Clark, a senior scholar at the Poynter Institute for Media Studies who has coauthored books with Fry, writes regularly about the craft of storytelling on the center's website (www.poynter.org/). In one essay, "Fifty Writing Tools: Quick List," he gives, as the title suggests, fifty tips on writing compelling sentences.[4] Several apply particularly well to the critical process of revising.

- Cut big, then small. Prune the big limbs, then shake out the dead leaves.
- Prefer the simple over the technical. Use shorter words, sentences, and paragraphs at points of complexity. [Twain once said, "I never write metropolis for seven cents because I can get the same price for city."[5]]
- Play with words, even in serious stories. Choose words the average writer avoids but the average reader understands.
- Seek original images. [Avoid clichés.]
- Tune your voice (read drafts aloud).

Revising, of course, never ensures perfection. It rarely, if ever, achieves it either. What it usually delivers is tauter, more vigorous prose.

Writers drafting on blank pages must create order and flow, neatly cadenced rows of paragraphs from unruly fields of information. The act of ordering this empty space can exhaust, depleting the energy needed to shape and prune each individual sentence.

CARVE TIME BETWEEN DRAFTS

When I can, I try to disengage, to sleep on first drafts, at least to stroll around the block. When I come back to the page I try to carry a sharp knife and a keen BS detector. Both have their place.

Revision, however, needn't rip up what's in place. Sometimes changes between drafts are subtle. Here are the first several paragraphs of a story I wrote about a French cooking class, with edits corresponding to the third draft I wrote before submitting the piece for publication (it ran in the *Christian Science Monitor*, with additional minor copyediting changes). Most changes here were minor additions or deletions. Deleted words have a strike through them, and additions are italicized and in bold face.

Third Draft

I know we cooked with generous quantities of onions, garlic, and olive oil, turning the chicken with a wooden spoon to avoid puncturing ~~the~~ *its* skin and releasing ~~the bird's~~ *its* natural juices.

I know that if madame said it once she ~~must have~~ said it a dozen times—presentation, particularly of the first course or entrée—counts as much as taste.

And I know that by the time we sat down to eat ~~our dinner~~ at 8:15 p.m., after two and a half hours of watching and listening and ~~smelling~~ *inhaling the meal's aroma, I was so hungry* my left sock might have tasted pretty good. Still, our family style meal provencale ("cuisine familiale," as our teacher, Madame Catherine Plan stressed) actually was delectable.

Whether I, with 10 left thumbs, and a cooking resume that ends after scrambled eggs, hamburgers en grille and deep-fried potatoes, could recreate any*thing* ~~of the delicious dishes~~ madame prepared. Well, that remains to be seen.

But for 25 Euros a person, the evening, organized by IS Aix-en-Provence, the international language school where we had begun our five-month adventure in France, still seemed a steal. It included the four-course meal, five hours of French conversation, nearly three hours of cooking instruction, and, of course, the chance to enjoy Madame Plan, who after 15 years of offering such evenings can slice and dice garlic and onions, stir a pot of chicken, mash a jar of olives for tapenade and keep up a steady stream of advice ~~and opinion~~ for five foreign onlookers without so much as adjusting her apron. (When she was done cooking the dishwasher was ~~already~~ loaded as well.)

QUESTIONS TO CONSIDER

As you revise your own work, start by asking these questions:

1. Have I read my work aloud? Does it sound like me?
2. Does each word serve a purpose? If not, which words do not?
3. Does the story track? Does it need any "street signs" or transitions to easily lead the reader from one idea to the next? Or does its structure allow the reader to transition naturally?
4. Do specific images and examples support each general statement?
5. Am I using language in fresh and original ways?

One of this country's better writers is our current president, Barack Obama. That was evident in the succinct, specific eulogy he delivered at the funeral of Massachusetts senator Ted Kennedy.

Its language built on nouns that captured Kennedy's many roles and verbs—active, simple, and original—that served as the speech's engine. Here is an excerpt with the active verbs italicized.

> Today we *say* goodbye to the youngest child of Rose and Joseph Kennedy. The world *will* long *remember* their son Edward as the heir to a weighty legacy; a champion for those who had none; the soul of the Democratic Party; and the lion of the United States Senate—a man whose name *graces* nearly 1,000 laws, and who *penned* more than 300 laws himself.
>
> But those of us who *loved* him, and *ache* with his passing, *know* Ted Kennedy by the other titles he *held*: Father. Brother. Husband. Uncle Teddy, or as he was often known to his younger nieces and nephews, "The Grand Fromage," or "the Big Cheese." I, like so many others in the city where he *worked* for nearly half a century, *knew* him as a colleague, a mentor, and above all, a friend.
>
> Ted Kennedy was the baby of the family who *became* its patriarch; the restless dreamer who *became* its rock. He was the sunny, joyful child, who *bore* the brunt of his brothers' teasing, but *learned* quickly how to *brush* it off. When they *tossed* him off a boat because he *didn't know* what a jib was, 6-year-old Teddy *got* back in and *learned* to sail. When a photographer *asked* the newly-elected Bobby to *step* back at a press conference because he was casting a shadow on his younger brother, Teddy *quipped*, "It'll be the same in Washington."[6]

Obama's words are meant to be heard. Long sentences follow short, some branching rightward from subject and adjoining verb, others changing cadence by ending with a strong verb or noun.

This sprit of resilience and good humor *would see* Ted Kennedy through more pain and tragedy than most of us *will* ever *know*. He *lost* two siblings by the age of 16. He *saw* two more taken violently from the country that *loved* them. He *said* goodbye to his beloved sister, Eunice, in the final days of his own life. He narrowly *survived* a plane crash, *watched* two children struggle with cancer, *buried* three nephews, and *experienced* personal failings and setbacks in the most public way possible.

It is a string of events that *would have broken* a lesser man. And it would have been easy for Teddy to *let* himself become bitter and hardened; to *surrender* to self-pity and regret; to *retreat* from public life and *live* out his years in peaceful quiet. No one *would have blamed* him for that.[7]

Its language appeals to the senses. "We can still *hear* his voice bellowing through the Senate chamber, face *reddened*, fist *pounding* the podium, a veritable force of nature, in support of health care or workers' rights or civil rights."

General thematic sentences, the transitions, set up new themes. Specific, concrete images and examples follow.

But though it is Ted Kennedy's historic body of achievements that we *will remember*, it is his giving heart that we *will miss*. It was the friend and colleague who was always the first to pick up the phone and say, "I'm sorry for your loss," or "I hope you feel better," or "What can I do to help?" It was the boss who was so *adored* by his staff that over five hundred spanning five decades *showed up* for his 75th birthday. It was the man who *sent* birthday wishes and thank you notes and even his own paintings to so many who never *imagined* that a U.S. Senator of such stature *would take* the time to *think* about someone like them.[8]

And in his juxtaposition of words and images describing Kennedy's character, Obama's language regularly surprises. "The greatest expectations were placed upon Ted Kennedy's shoulders because of who he was, but he *surpassed* them because of who he *became*."

It was a beautiful eulogy, one the president had clearly spent considerable time writing—and likely multiple drafts. Good writing demands that, even from a president.

At the end of chapter 13, you should have completed a draft of a friend's, colleague's, or family member's story about a challenge he or she confronted and overcame. Now your task is to revise that draft. I'd recommend these steps:

1. Read your piece aloud, marking any place that your tongue trips. Return to those marks and ask why.
   a. Should the sentence be split in two?
   b. Should it be recast in the active voice (subject-verb-object construction)?
   c. Is the sentence's punctuation clear?
   d. Does it start or end strong, or are the strongest elements buried in midsentence?
   e. Is the language simple or bloated by efforts to sound important?
2. In a different color pen, identify the story's key points.
   a. Does your story have a framework that progresses logically?
   b. Is it organized by theme, place, time, or in some other manner?
   c. Does it double back in any way?
   d. Are like ideas kept together?
3. Look closely at the story's content.
   a. Do you have specific anecdotes, examples, and scenes to support general statements?
   b. Have you left material in your notes that would show the story better than what you've included?
   c. Are there gaps in your reporting or understanding?
4. Force yourself to trim at least 10 percent of the words and preferably 20 percent.
   a. Can you do so without losing content or meaning?
   b. What adjectives (modifying nouns) and adverbs (modifying verbs) remain in the story. Why? Can you eliminate adverbs by using more precise verbs?
   c. Can you save space by eliminating prepositional phrases, choosing more specific words, or being more succinct?

Once you are done, take a walk or cook a meal. Then read your story aloud again.

FIFTEEN
FINDING A NICHE

Caitlin Kelly had a substantial newspaper reporting career behind her in Canada and the United States when she sold her memoir. Still, it was only then that she discovered how fast the world of publishing is changing. "My agent told me in no uncertain language that when you [write] a book now, you have to blog or publishers won't take you seriously. . . . It is a tool to—I hate this language—to build your brand. These days if you don't build your brand, you disappear."

On July 1, 2009, Kelly began blogging at the hub *True/Slant*, which had signed up freelance writers ranging from journalists to college professors, psychologists, and fitness specialists. She hadn't had much interest in blogs before. But she took to her new work like a Labrador retriever introduced to water, becoming one of the site's most prolific "posters" within months.

"One of the things I find about blogging is that people react, which is very, very different from journalism," she said toward the end of the year. "Journalism is like spitting down a well. You have no way of knowing if anyone read any of it. . . . You'd like someone to say, 'That's interesting. Let's talk about that.' If you're lucky maybe someone in your newsroom says, 'good job.' . . . With blogging there is this fascinating [interaction]." She's also found that blogging has opened up new dimensions in her writing. "It's so freeing and so different." Kelly knew she'd need to cultivate this looser, more personal style in writing a memoir.

The changing landscape of storytelling can be daunting, particularly for today's professionals. Print newspaper and magazine circulation and advertising have plummeted, leading to layoffs, reduced salaries, and sharp reductions in well-paid, freelance work. New forms of writing, often shorter, sassier, interlinked, and multimedia, are emerging online. And no one who is honest can predict what's next.

"I suspect that until our brains are radically rewired, text is going to be a big part of things," says Joshua Benton, director of Harvard University's Nieman Journalism Lab, billed as "an attempt to help journalism figure out its future in an Internet age."

"The biggest change we're already seeing," he adds, "is that artificial publishing schedules of newspapers and especially magazines, where stories get told in one big chunk, is [changing]. I think what we're already seeing in forms like blogging is the possibility of stories being told in real time and over time."

For professionals like Kelly, the blogosphere is a chance to experiment with new forms. It's also a place to be read, be seen, and supplement a paycheck as she and other writers navigate through changing times. For new writers, the blogosphere offers an exceptional opportunity to build a presence, practice craft, and establish who they are.

C. C. Chapman is a sort of self-made marketing and new media guy. He says he'd never try to pass himself off as a journalist, and yet his website, www.cc-chapman.com, offers an eclectic mix of blog posts, podcasts, and photography, one man's contribution to the varied storytelling of the twenty-first century. Last year, he started a new site called Digital Dads, which he'd like to build into "a destination for fathers to post and get content." He already has more than five hundred "followers."

What Chapman knows a lot about, and Kelly is learning, is how to build a personal brand. "The only thing standing in your way in terms of writing is yourself," Chapman advises the new writer. "To be a writer, you've got to write. You've got to constantly be providing new content for people to notice you. . . . First and foremost you've got to establish a personal website for yourself online. Have a presence on Facebook and Twitter. Make sure you're up on Linked-In. Make it impossible for people not to find you (and your work)."

Still others have used regular or daily blog posts as building blocks for books, layered step by step in short personal narrative. In 2009, Meryl Streep fans flocked to *Julie and Julia,* a charming bit of character acting in which Streep becomes Julia Child, the audacious American in Paris who taught herself about French cooking and then wrote a best-selling book, *Mastering the Art of French Cooking,* for Americans. The film, however, interwove two stories. In the second, actress Amy Adams portrayed Julie Powell, a real and frustrated writer who in 2004 blogged incessantly about her exhausting quest to cook all 521 recipes in Child's famous book in a single year.

The real Powell then sold a book, *Julie and Julia: My Year of Cooking Dangerously,* based on her blog and experience.[1] In a review, *Publishers Weekly* noted, "Some passages . . . are taken verbatim from the blog, but Powell expands on her experience." The review called her writing "feisty and unrestrained," a nice reflection of the tone of the blogosphere.[2]

Also in 2009, Colin Beavan published a book, *No Impact Man,*[3] built from his blog chronicling a yearlong attempt to diminish his environmental impact on the planet to near zero. He continued to blog on the subject, posting this on December 18, 2009:

Since the release of the *No Impact Man* book and film I have been privileged to be in conversation with many groups. And always, someone asks me with great earnestness, "What can I do?" Many times, in other words, people ask me for how-to-save-the-planet directions.

"Just start," I say.

And then I pause while they wait expectantly for more guidance.

"If you were to just start, without waiting for someone like me to come along, what would you do?" I ask finally.

. . . there is another pause.

Finally, I might say, "Look to yourself for guidance. What would you like to do?"

And then a person might say: "I'd like to start riding my bike to work" or "I'd like to campaign against bottled water" or "I'd like to start a compost pile in my building" or "I'd like to tell people we should love each other more."

Then I laugh. "So why are you asking me what you can do? Just start."

Most of us already know.

We know. *You* know.[4]

JUST START

As its title implies, this final chapter of this book is intended to give you some tips on how to position yourself for a writing career in the twenty-first century. But most of you, as Beavan says, already know: you need to write, revise, establish your voice, and publish your work for others to see it. You need to "just start."

Granted, these are tough times for writers to earn a big paycheck. But it's a remarkably easy one for them to begin publishing their work. Choose your free, blogging software (I've used Blogspot, then switched to WordPress) and you're off.

Along the way, experiment. In his wonderful talk at the 2008 Nieman Narrative Journalism Conference, Joshua Benton referred to bloggers and more polished, long-form narrative journalists as compatriots in the battle to tell stories instead of file news reports in the overregimented style of newspaper bland. He used this food metaphor to make his point: "If you think of narrative journalism as a beautiful French pastry. . . . Blogging is the rustic farmer's loaf. . . . We are both fighting the Wonderbread in the middle. We are both attacking the sort of tasteless, over-processed style that dominates our unfortunate dying publications."[5]

BUILDING A BRAND

All the young writers I've met face the same dilemma. When they seek experience—try to sell their first piece or get their first job, they are told to get some experience first. That, of course, is exactly what they're trying to do. It's an age-old conundrum. And it's one the Internet can help solve.

"Every person has to be at peace with the idea that you have to promote yourself," Benton says. "It will mean having your own web site. It will mean being active in social media. . . . It will mean figuring out who you are."He offers these tips:

- Register your Web domain, using your name. ("JoshuaBenton.com is not my blog," he said. But he does own it.)
- Work to establish multiple entries on the Web to your name so that you become the first person on a Google search to pop up under that name. You'll increase your chances by having a blog, a Facebook page, a Twitter account, a Google profile, and a Linked-In account, as well as by signing up for other networking opportunities as they develop.
- Get a respectable and clear e-mail account (not hotdog@aol.com).
- Start writing "and do it in public . . . the freedom that comes with suddenly having an audience of people is a glorious thing. There are lots of folks around the Internet who have really blossomed once they've decided to have a blog."
- Think about your audience and what you can contribute to it: develop a niche. For Benton, a Louisianan and a Cajun, that niche, when he began his blog *crabwalk.com* more than a decade ago, was often to write about Cajuns and Louisiana history—even though he had a day job as a reporter writing about other issues.
- Be a good citizen. "Be respectful, reach out to others, leave productive comments on other people's stuff," Benton says. "Good behavior tends to be rewarded two or three times over."

Networking (which in the end is what good citizenship results in) can pay off down the road, as well, because it can lead to work and to contacts if eventually you decide to reach out to professional editors for an assignment and a conventional means of being paid for your work.

SELLING YOUR WORK

Just as the blogosphere has made storytelling forms less convention bound, e-mail has changed the nature of *pitching* or *querying* stories. Plenty of books still circulate about the formal query letter. Sent by old-fashioned snail mail, its goal was to sell story and writer in the first sentence and paragraph; lay out a proposal's focus—something like a nut graf—in its second or third; tantalize with selective details supporting that focus; and introduce the writer before signing off. The rule of thumb is that every query has to make its point and pitch in a single page or less, though writers sometimes stretch that in pitches to editors with whom they have a working relationship.

Here is an example of a traditional query, compliments of my colleague Jeffrey Seglin, a professor of magazine publishing at Emerson, a syndicated business ethics columnist, and a former editor at *Inc.*, a magazine covering small business. It was written to a newspaper by his son-in-law, David Whitemyer, an architect who also freelances.

> Dear _____,
> While working in the garden one sunny Saturday morning, my pre-school-age son pulled an earthworm from the soil and asked, "Dad, can I kill it?" In a flash, my mind filled with thoughts of ecological destruction, Jainism, DSS, and the Columbine massacre.
> I fumbled my words and said, "Sure Buddy, go ahead."
> In hindsight, I would've said something else, maybe explained how worms aerate the soil. I'm not sure. But I've been mulling this over a lot lately, and I am interested in writing an essay for ___ on the topic. Respecting the fact that "boys will be boys" and that toying with small creatures is part of growing up, I'm still conflicted as to what the correct response is to "can I kill it?"
> The essay would focus on my wavering confusion. Buddhism says, "No." And our politically correct culture assumes that there's a connection between experimental animal torture and the next Littleton. Still, the Dad in me keeps looking at this as normal juvenile development. And it's hard for me to preach about the ills of insect murder when I'm spraying ant poison around the perimeter of the house.
> I am a frequent contributor to _____.
> Thanks very much for your time.

I liked this query. It showed the writer's humanity, his sense of humor, and his essay's purpose. It's written in a conversational tone. Its point is clear. But Whitemyer didn't sell this piece. Freelancing is always a crapshoot. Perhaps he needed to touch on the advice of an "expert." Maybe he would have made headway by following up with a phone call to brainstorm the idea further with an editor. Quite possibly, had he sent the pitch to a parenting magazine rather than a general-interest newspaper, his odds would have improved.

Audience matters. Certainly Whitemyer knew better than to pitch his piece to *Fortune*, a business magazine, or to *Vogue*, a fashion magazine. Articles have to fit both the publication and the niche within that publication. And writers need to research in advance what else the magazine or newspaper has written about a topic.

   In his query, Whitemyer also might have indicated how long his piece would be though he had written for the publication before. A newcomer always wants to tip the editor that he knows the publication's length constraints.

THE ENDLESS WAIT

In pre-Internet days, the wait for a query answer could be interminable. (Often, of course, no answer came.) Back then, I was always taught to end with a sentence saying, "I look forward to hearing from you. If I haven't heard from you in two weeks I'll follow up with a phone call." (That was a polite way of saying, "Don't try to weasel out on me. If you don't bother answering, I'll hunt you down.")

   Today, in an age of e-mail, queries are quicker and less formal. Now, as then, they have a much better chance of success for the writer who has networked, met the editor, gotten an introduction from a friend of the editor, or in some other way laid the groundwork for a letter or e-mail so it doesn't appear to arrive from outer space.

   Here's an excerpt from a query I sent from France to Judy Lowe, an editor at the *Christian Science Monitor* for whom I'd written slice-of-life and travel pieces before. I'm old school, so it stayed fairly close to traditional query structure (the article I wrote is excerpted in chapter 3, "Culling Life's Experience").

   Driving southeast from Carcassonne, France, on the narrow, two-lane D611, triangular signs with images of falling black boulders line the route. I'm never quite sure how to guard against these rock slides but the signs do scare me into gripping the wheel of our gray Ford putt-putt hard with both hands.

   This is windblown, hardscrabble country with outcroppings of crumbling rock and dry canyon creeks reminiscent of the Eastern slope of the Colorado Rockies. But here in the province of Languedoc, you can drive for kilometers and see no sign of life other than an occasional patch of thirsty vineyard or the odd hand-lettered sign alerting drivers that "Jesus, t'aime (Jesus loves you)."

   Turn west onto D14 and the land gets hillier, more forested, more dramatic. This is where, in the 13th century, the Cathars fought and lost to the Christian crusaders—often in bloody massacres—and where, during the four centuries that followed, the warriors of France guarded what was then the southern border of France against incursions from Aragon, an area now divided between portions of Spain's Catalonia and France. Today, we are on the trail of these knights and the Cathar ghosts before

them, driving between and scrambling up rocks to massive fortifica-
tion remnants 1,000 years old and more.

I propose an 800-word article, "On the Road of the Cathars," that
takes would-be tourists into this dramatic landscape and shares a bit of
its history. Adding to the drama and trauma of this experience was my
own tour guide and map nut, my wife Kathy, who ended our day by
leading me down a single-lane road with two-lane traffic, overhanging
a canyon. I have plenty of pictures of the castles, landscape and road,
though I realize you may prefer file art. Should you be looking for any
sort of news peg, the final castle we visited holds four days of jousting
and merriment in mid-August, a perfect time for visitors.

Best,

Jerry

Less formal still is this query from Jina Moore, a talented young *Monitor* freelancer, to Clara Germani, a senior editor who assigns, develops, and edits the cover stories of the *Monitor*'s weekly magazine. Here is an excerpt, which shows something of the writer's style as well as the story's content. (Once again, the writer knew the editor.)

Hi Clara,

Here's an idea that I think might make a good cover story: development
tourism. I've been wanting to write about this since I went to Sierra Le-
one, where tourism chat boards were populated with people looking for
a nice beach stay for two days, and a project to volunteer at. . . . But I've
found something even better.

There's a company here called New Dawn Associates that promotes
"responsible tourism" and has a package of "educational tours" you can
take. You can go out to rural Rwanda and watch the pygmies throw pots,
or slip down to the southern part of the country and learn about the ancient Rwandan art of cow dung paintings.

The initiatives are both to educate the slightly more erudite tourists
(and lots of delegations from any number of professions) and to protect
the culture of the people they're seeing. . . .

The questions at the heart of this story are actually important: Does this
bring these people real revenue? (There's a whole money-sharing scheme
allegedly in place.) How does that make a difference in their lives?

In a way, the writer here is saying, "Here's the news and here's why I
think you should care," a technique we talked about in focusing stories
earlier in this book. And she's saying it with a bit of style.

"I really like someone who has talent and can write a conversational pitch," Germani says. "If a cover letter has some humor in it or just some flair that catches my eye and says to me that person has confidence." However, it is most important to Germani that the cover letter establishes a focus. "If I see something in their pitch that verges on a nut graf, I say, 'Ah, this is what they're going to build their story around.' I like the synthesis of the nut graf in the middle. What it all means, what the theme is."

DOS AND DON'TS

Ultimately, Germani warns, selling and developing a good article involves much more than simply sending a compelling pitch or query. A good letter might get her to the phone to talk to an unfamiliar writer. But rarely if ever does she issue a contract without much more extensive developmental work. Writers, she cautions, should always be prepared for the follow-up brainstorming session if an idea catches an editor's interest.

"Most of the people who are good I end up having a personal or at least professional relationship with," Germani says. "I hear their voice. I can tell whether or not they have confidence in that voice about something. I can also tell when they're talking off the top of their head."

Relationship building has always been behind the art of selling freelance work. Germani encourages would-be writers to get in touch with her before they head off to a faraway place that might well interest the *Christian Science Monitor*, a news organization with a strong commitment to international reporting.

"I never say no to lunch or coffee," Germani says. "And people forget about that today because it's all e-mail. E-mail is really easy to ignore. If by some chance (someone) sends a pitch and the pitch is good but it's not what I need in the moment, they'll never get my attention. But if they say, 'I'm so-and-so, and I'm going to Liberia for six months,' I'll always see them. I'll remember who they are, and I'll have a softer place for them in my heart after I've met them."

Phone calls, she warns, can catch an editor at a bad time and easily be forgotten. Instead, she suggests, it's better to invite the editor to coffee. All she can do is say no. Dropping the name of a common acquaintance doesn't hurt either. Journalists move in a small universe; and those who inhabit it often start conversations by seeing whom they know in common. A would-be freelancer shouldn't hide, for example, that "I wrote for Anderson in college, and he speaks highly of you. Please feel free to call him about my work."

If writers can help their cause, they can also hurt it. Editors, or their assistants, will immediately discard queries written to an editor who quit six months ago, or sent to someone whose name is misspelled or title mangled. Such errors reflect carelessness on the part of the writer. And an editor working with freelancers wants above all to be able to trust them.

Queries cast as multiple-page treatises are also dead on arrival. Remember the proposal I sent Lowe about the Cathars? Had I started with five paragraphs about the history and culture of the Cathars I'd likely have never heard back from her. She'd have known my topic but had no idea what I wanted to say about it.

Writers who are glib or oversell their stories also raise red flags, Germani said. She recalled one recent pitch in which the would-be freelancer boasted that he had "a very good chance of interviewing Obama." Now that's overselling.

Finally, Germani said, would-be writers stumble when they don't know the publication, its values, its style, or what it's written recently. Pitching an article requires homework about not only the topic but also the place the writer wants to sell it. Fairly regularly, Germani says, she gets pitches about local programs in the city of Boston. "They think because we're in Boston, we're interested in Boston. That just doesn't go anywhere." Why not? Because the *Monitor* is a national and international publication.

And now, for a final time, it's your turn. It's time to try to publish that article you've been writing and refining. But before you build a blog site and pop it on, let's try to find a broader audience. Ask yourself these questions.

1. What kind of audience might want to read my story?
2. What publications cater to such audiences? (A good place to find out is in the book *Writer's Market*,[6] which can be found at any good-sized public library.)

Research the publication, reviewing what it has written on your subject, what section seems most likely to consider it, and what length meets the publication's guidelines. Call to check who the appropriate section editor is (never rely on a name in a book to send a pitch letter or a resume; editors change regularly). If the publication is close to your home, call or e-mail the editor to see if you can meet her or him for coffee. Use this time to simply get acquainted. Don't be heavy handed about pushing your idea.

   Craft a query that follows the chapter's guidelines. Keep it to a page. Make sure it's specific. And use it to sell your story and yourself. (Tip: Many editors react badly to being sent unsolicited manuscripts. Try to get a sense of this, but if you're unsure send a query instead.)

   What are your odds of selling your first piece? Not good, particularly in today's climate. But by then perhaps you'll have set up your own "publication." I'll see you in the blogosphere.

Postscript

In the more than three years since I began this book, the blogosphere, social media, and other technological innovations—and those who take advantage of all three—have driven a revolution in publishing, journalism, and communication that some serious people I know are comparing to the invention of the printing press. Is this hyperbole? I'll leave that to historians. But this I do know. As much as professional writers lament that it's becoming harder to scratch a sustainable living, "citizen journalists" and other self-publishers are finding—and using—ways to tell stories that have never before been available to them. I hope this book has inspired you to join the tens of millions who are already exercising their voices online and who've already begun telling stories, their own and others.

Interestingly, the blogosphere may bring on the resurgence of another lost art in this age of Tweets and Instant Chat: letter writing. Historians sift through letters to reveal the past. Yet, who takes the time today to put quill, or even ballpoint, to paper and write to friends or loved ones? Mary Wiltenburg is one. Using bits and bytes instead of ink, she ended her yearlong series, or at least its regular blog, with a letter to Bill and Igey, the boys aged nine and seven, whom she followed through a year at the International Community School in Atlanta after their family resettled there from a Tanzanian refugee camp. Here is some of what she wrote.

Dear Bill and Igey,

When we first met, I wondered if you would grow up to read these stories. Your teachers were worried about you learning to read, and neither of you had really seen the Internet, so it seemed like it would be a long time before that happened.

But this year, you surprised everyone. Suddenly, your parents weren't the only ones who realized how smart and funny you are. Your teachers could see it. Your friends could see it. People following these stories saw it and cared about you from across the world. And you boys not only started reading—you started going online, then on friends' Facebook pages. I know now that you will see all of this much sooner than I imagined.

So as this project ends today, I want to tell you how lucky I feel to have spent this year with you. There were tough times along the way, for your family, for your school, and especially for your sister. Bill, I know you didn't always enjoy all the photos and questions and attention. Thank you for being patient with me anyway.

Lots of moments from the past year still crack me up: When we talked about Michael Jackson, or kissing, or the origin of the world, or life in your old refugee camp. Igey, you are hilarious even when drugged [he underwent minor surgery].

In serious moments, I was struck by how caring you both are. One day this summer, Igey, you called me to say that three chicks had fallen out of their nest. You had rescued them, scooped them onto a paper towel, and hidden them under your bed to keep them safe. But they were chirping, and hungry, and you didn't know where to find worms.

I didn't either, so we settled for bread. . . . When they were full, you climbed the tree they had fallen out of and put them back in a new nest made of a cardboard box.

It seemed unlikely to work, and I tried to prepare you. But when we checked later that day, there was the mother bird, bustling around her boxful of babies. You were beside yourselves with joy, dancing around the parking lot shouting: "She's back! The mama! The mama is back!"

The other night, Igey, you called again worried about the future. We talked about years from now, when you go to high school, and you asked: "Will we still know each other then?"

I said of course we will.

And you said: "But will you still come to my house?"

I hope so. I'm proud to know both of you, and always will be.

Love, Mary

For Wiltenburg, the letter was a chance to leave her young subjects with a memory, a postscript of her series. So, I thought I'd leave you with a postscript from, and for, our household as well. Kathy and I returned to Aix-en-Provence, France, in the summer of 2010, finding it just as enchanting—and idiosyncratic—as the first time around. At times, we talk of retiring there. We arrived home to meet our first grandson, Dylan, born to our older daughter, Betsy, on July 2.

As for Devon, that grandchild whose arrival in summer 2007 wrenched us back to the realities of aging and the responsibilities of parents, time has more than salved any sense of uncertainty. She's nearly three now, a frequent and much-anticipated visitor at our house. And, of course, I am still writing about her, in blogs that sometimes stay in the privacy of my own home, in blogs, and, once, in an article for traditional news media. She no longer paralyzes my writing process either. She enriches it—along with my life. I wrote this blog about her and her new partner in havoc for *True/Slant* on December 15, 2009.

When I walk through the kitchen door at night, Murphy wiggles and sometimes turns in circles four or five times. When Devon walks through the kitchen door weekend mornings, she heads straight to the bottom of the stairs and yells up to me, "Ada, get off the computer."

Murphy is my son, sort of; he's our third golden retriever. Devon is my granddaughter.

I'm starting to think that finally, in my 60th year, I've learned a few things that are letting me do a better job with dogs and kids alike.

Take Murphy. He's never met another dog he doesn't like. That wasn't true of our first two goldens, who loved people but sometimes, with me nervously tugging their leashes, mixed it up with other dogs. The difference is that Murphy meets his friends on his own terms, off leash.

It's a lesson Kathy and I learned under duress. Murphy had a few problems as a puppy. He surfed counter tops for food, barked incessantly when he wasn't in the same room, ate anything that fit in his mouth. But he was at his worst when it came time to walk on a leash. He growled. He grabbed it in his mouth. Sometimes he bit at our clothes.

Kathy rubbed Bitter Apple on the leash. Didn't work. We tried a chain leash. Too heavy. Finally, we hired a personal trainer. She told us to buy a pronged collar and jerk it when the dog didn't follow commands. That's when Murphy really went nuts. In desperation, we fired the trainer, stuffed our pockets with cheese, and began taking Murphy off leash to conservation land, figuring, if he ran away, it would just prove his insanity. And we introduced tennis balls to his life.

Today, at 18 months, Murphy is a prince. Among his friends, he can count Monet, the rescued golden; Nikki, the speedy mixed breed; and Benny, the little whippersnapper who humps everything in sight. He chews for hours on tennis balls instead of sticks, plastic, furniture or the kitchen wall, in which he dug a 2-foot-in-diameter hole when he was three months old. His energy spent, his friendships firmly established, he relaxes and walks better on a leash, too. And he's stopped barking.

For her part, Devon, who is 2, has never needed much more discipline than a hug, a nap routine and occasional deflection when stuck in "no" mode. Here I've learned, too. As a grandparent, all I do is revel in her company. I don't test her, so she doesn't need to test me. I don't push her, so she doesn't need to push back. Often it seems that simple.

At times Meg, who is an amazing single mom, reaches the end of her rope. I've seen her get bossy.

"Devon, if you don't eat any dinner, I'm taking away your Elmo DVD."

Now that is a threat.

Devon digs in. Meghan digs in. No one wins.

And then my past flashes back, the father of that rebellious teenage girl who wanted a friend in her confused adolescence and got an angry Dad, fighting a losing battle to impose rules that sometimes had little reason.

Sometimes it takes a few times around to get things right. This much I've figured out. Dogs need freedom; kids need unconditional love. And neither alpha dogs nor alpha dads really lead the pack.

NOTES

PREFACE

1. Phillip Winn, "State of the Blogosphere 2008: Introduction," Technorati, August 21, 2009, at http://technorati.com/blogging/article/state-of-the-blogosphere-introduction (accessed July 12, 2010).

2. Amanda Lenhart and Susannah Fox, "Bloggers: A Portrait of the Internet's New Storytellers," Pew Internet and American Life Project, July 19, 2006, at www.pewinternet.org/~/media/Files/Reports/2006/PIP%20Bloggers%20Report%20July%2019%202006.pdf.pdf (accessed July 12, 2010).

3. Amanda Lenhart, Kristen Purcell, Aaron Smith, and Kathryn Zickuhr, "Social Media and Young Adults," Pew Internet and American Life Project, February 3, 2010, at www.pewinternet.org/Reports/2010/Social-Media-and-Young-Adults.aspx (accessed July 12, 2010).

CHAPTER 1: FINDING A PLACE—AND SPACE—TO THINK

1. Anne Lamott, *Bird by Bird: Some Instructions on Writing and Life* (New York: Anchor Books, 1995), xxvi.

2. William Zinsser, *On Writing Well: The Classic Guide to Writing Nonfiction*, 25th anniversary ed. (New York: Quill, 2001), 49.

CHAPTER 2: A LITTLE JAZZ

1. Peter Elbow, *Writing with Power: Techniques for Mastering the Writing Process* (New York: Oxford University Press, 1998), 13.

CHAPTER 3: CULLING LIFE'S EXPERIENCE

1. Zinsser, *On Writing Well*, 5.
2. Lenhart and Fox, "Bloggers."

3. Adam Gopnik, *Paris to the Moon* (New York: Random House, 2000), 15.

CHAPTER 4: GATHERING STRING

1. Walt Harrington, ed., *Intimate Journalism: The Art and Craft of Reporting Everyday Life* (Thousand Oaks, Calif.: Sage, 1999), xiv.

CHAPTER 5: THE PASSIVE OBSERVER AT WORK

1. Tom Wolfe, *The Right Stuff* (New York: Farrar, Straus and Giroux, 1979), 212.
2. Tom Wolfe, *The New Journalism* (New York: Harper & Row, 1973), 15.

CHAPTER 6: FINDING FRESH STORIES

1. William E. Blundell, *The Art and Craft of Feature Writing: Based on the* Wall Street Journal *Guide* (New York: New American Library, 1988), x.
2. Jon Franklin, *Writing for Story: Craft Secrets of Dramatic Nonfiction by a Two-Time Pulitzer Prize Winner* (New York: Plume, 1994), 78.

CHAPTER 7: RECONNAISSANCE

1. Zinsser, *On Writing Well*, 52.
2. Blundell, *The Art and Craft of Feature Writing*, 70.
3. Blundell, *The Art and Craft of Feature Writing*, 84.

CHAPTER 8: HONING THE FOCUS

1. Carl Sessions Stepp, *Writing as Craft and Magic* (Lincolnwood, Ill.: NTC Publishing Group, 2000), 46.

CHAPTER 9: INTERVIEWING FOR STORY

1. Anna Quindlen, "Hers," *New York Times*, April 10, 1986.
2. Jay Black, Bob Steele, Ralph Barney, *Doing Ethics in Journalism: A Handbook with Case Studies*, 3rd ed. (Boston: Allyn and Bacon, 1999), 33–36.

CHAPTER 10: BRING BACK THE BREED OF THE DOG

1. Adam Moss, "Hot Properties: Reinventing New York and Relaunching the Web Site," *New York Magazine*, September 26, 2009.

2. Donald Fry, quoted in *America's Best Newspaper Writing: A Collection of ASNE Prizewinners*, comp. Roy Peter Clark and Christopher Scanlan, 2nd ed. (Boston: Bedford/St. Martin's, 2006).

3. Gay Talese, "A Conversation with Gay Talese," at "The Power of Narrative: Timeless Art in an Urgent Age" Narrative Journalism Conference, Boston University, Friday, April 23, 2010.

CHAPTER 12: DRAFTING FAST

1. Lamott, *Bird by Bird*, 22.

CHAPTER 13: ORGANIZING STORIES

1. Franklin, *Writing for Story*, 71.

2. Tom Hallman, quoted in *Best Newspaper Writing 1997*, ed. Christopher Scanlan (St. Petersburg, Fla.: Poynter Institute for Media Studies, 1997), 60.

3. Stepp, *Writing as Craft and Magic*, 223.

4. Zinsser, *On Writing Well*, 71.

CHAPTER 14: NO ONE GETS IT RIGHT THE FIRST TIME

1. Mark Twain, letter to George Bainton, October 15, 1888, Mark Twain House and Museum, Hartford, Conn., at http://marktwainhouse.blogspot. com/2009_04_01_archive.html (accessed July 19, 2010).

2. William Strunk Jr. and E. B. White, *The Elements of Style*, 50th anniversary ed. (New York: Pearson Longman, 2009).

3. Donald Fry, quoted in *Writing Tools: 50 Essential Strategies for Every Writer*, by Roy Peter Clark (New York: Little, Brown, 2006), 112.

4. Roy Peter Clark, "Fifty Writing Tools: Quick List," June 30, 2006, at www. poynter.org/column.asp?id=78&aid=103943 (accessed July 19, 2010).

5. Alex Ayres, ed., *The Wit and Wisdom of Mark Twain* (New York: Perennial, 2005), 252.

6. Barack Obama, eulogy for Senator Ted Kennedy, Our Lady of Perpetual Help Basilica, Boston, August 29, 2009.

7. Obama, eulogy.

8. Obama, eulogy.

CHAPTER 15: FINDING A NICHE

1. Julie Powell, *Julie and Julia: My Year of Cooking Dangerously* (New York: Back Bay Books, 2009).

2. *Publishers Weekly*, "Julie and Julia: 365 Days, 524 Recipes, 1 Tiny Apartment Kitchen," review, June 13, 2005.

3. Colin Beavan, *No Impact Man* (New York: Farrar, Straus and Giroux, 2009).

4. Colin Beavan, "Trust the Spark Within and Find Your Own Path," No Impact Man, December 18, 2009, at http://noimpactman.typepad.com/blog/2009/12/trust-the-spark-within-and-find-your-own-path.html (accessed July 20, 2010).

5. Joshua Benton, "Blogging for Story," presented at the Nieman Narrative Journalism Conference, Boston, March 15, 2008.

6. Robert Lee Brewer, *Writer's Market 2010* (Cincinnati, Ohio: Writer's Digest Books, 2009).

Writing Examples

Many of the writing samples in the pages that follow are my own, in part because this is a book about my struggles and strategies for overcoming writer's block. Throughout, however, I have also leaned on writers more accomplished than I for examples that show the craft and mastery of nonfiction storytelling and the research and reporting behind it. These range from Gay Talese and a snippet of his classic *Esquire* profile, "Frank Sinatra Has a Cold," to some of the most recent winners of the Pulitzer Prize in Journalism, the profession's most prestigious award.

In a few cases, I have reprinted significant portions of stories or stories in their entirety. These are republished with the appropriate permissions. In others, I've merely taken a paragraph or two example. Regardless, I would like to thank all the publishers and writers from whose work I've drawn.

NEWSPAPERS

Boston Globe
Christian Science Monitor
International Herald Tribune
Mercury News (San Jose, Calif.)
New York Herald Tribune
New York Times
Post-Standard (Syracuse, N.Y.)
Spokesman-Review (Spokane, Wash.)
St. Paul Pioneer Press Dispatch (masthead at time piece was published)
Times-Picayune (New Orleans)
USA Today
Wall Street Journal
Washington Post

MAGAZINES

Esquire
New Yorker
Rolling Stone
Westchester Magazine

WEB PAGES

Csmonitor.com
Noimpactman.typepad.com/blog
Trueslant.com

Index

About the Author

Jerry Lanson is associate professor in Emerson College's Department of Journalism and was the department's first chair from 1999 to 2005. He is the coauthor of two books, *Writing and Reporting the News* (third edition) and *News in a New Century*, and writes a blog called Newsprints. Before coming to Emerson, Lanson served on the journalism faculties of New York University, Boston University, San Francisco State University, and Syracuse University. He is a former enterprise editor, bureau chief, special beats editor, deputy city editor, and acting city editor at the *San Jose Mercury News* and was part of the city-desk staff awarded a Pulitzer Prize for general news reporting in 1990. He has coached writers at regional and national conferences and a dozen newspapers, including the *Christian Science Monitor*, the *Boston Globe*, the *Portland Oregonian*, and the *San Jose Mercury News*. Lanson received Emerson College's teaching award in 2008–2009 and, in 1983, was one of ten journalism faculty members nationwide to receive a teaching award from the Poynter Institute for Media Studies in St. Petersburg, Florida. His blog can be found at jerrylanson.wordpress.com.